Navigating Successful Job Transitions

The Best Way to Find Your Next Job

agile.careers

Copyright • 2010 by Scott Uhrig. No part of this publication may be reproduced, stored in a retrieval system, or transmitted in any form without the written permission of Scott Uhrig or Career Artisan, 2412 McCall Road, Austin, TX 78703.

Introduction 9

1 - Somehow I Became a Headhunter 10
The Legend of David Baldwin 10
Can You Help Me Find a Job? 13
Learn How to Fish for Yourself 15

2 - Overview 16

3 - Get the Most Out of This Program 18
1 - Invest the Time 19
2 - Resist the Mighty Marshmallow 19
3 - Give Yourself Enough Runway 19
4 - Manage the Ups and Downs 20
5 - Keep Score 20
6 - Enlist the Support of Others 21

4 - Reflection Questions 22

Notes 23

Module 1 - Rethink 27

1 - Rethink Career Management 29
Agility is the New Stability 31
Embrace the Lowly Job Search 33

2 - Rethink the Job Search 34
No One Taught You How 34
Network, Network, Network 35
The Strength of Weak Ties 35
Job Search Alignment 36
The Sweet Spot 37
Do You Know of Any Good Jobs? 39

3 - Reflection Questions 42

Notes 43

Module 2 - Review and Reflect 47

1 - Where Have You Been? 50
2 - The Career Inventory Exercise 51
Professional Experience 51
Educational Experience 53
Other Experience 53
Summary Questions 53
3 - Capture Your Values 55
The Paradox of More 56
A Simple Framework for Career Success 61
4 - The Career Success Exercise 63
Reflection Questions 63
Values Identification 64
Values Clarification and Prioritization 64
Extra Credit 64
5 - Career Success Worksheet 65
6 - Capture Your Experience 66
7 - The Career Experience Exercise 70
8 - Career Experience Worksheet 71
9 - Career Experience Example 72
10 - Capture Your Market Value 73
11 - The Compensation History Exercise 74
12 - Compensation History Worksheet 75
Notes 76

Module 3 - Focus 79

1 - The Tao of Focus 81
2 - Explore 83
Narrow Your Geographic Focus 84
Complete Up To Three Target Job Profiles 85
Research the Jobs Online 85
Research the Jobs by Talking to People 86

Conduct Experiential Research if Necessary 87
Sanity Check the Market Size 87
3 - Make a Decision 89
Notes 91

Module 4 - Prepare to Launch 95
Job Search Alignment Redux 95
1 - Start Building Your Lists 97
When in Doubt, Start with One Company 100
But What if I'm Stuck? 101
2 - Write a Good Enough Resume 102
3 - Elevate Your Pitch 108
Your online persona 109
4 - Bonus 1: Working With Headhunters 111
How Recruiters Work 111
How to Best Leverage Recruiters 113
Recruiter Rules of Thumb 114
5 - Bonus 2: Using Online Job Sites 116
How Online Job Sites Work 116
How to Best Leverage Online Job Sites 116
6 - Target List Exercise 118
7 - Target Company List Example 119
8 - Target Company List Worksheet 120
9 - Target People List Example 121
10 - Target People List Worksheet 122
Notes 123

Module 5 - Execute 127
1 - Run a Process 128
Step 1 - Find Out as Much as You Can About the Company 129
Step 2 - Develop a Point of View (PoV) as to Where and How You Fit 132
Step 3 - Identify Specific Hiring Managers and Influencers 133

Step 4 - Network Your Way Into the Company and Connect With Hiring Managers 135

Networking Strategy - Who to Talk to and Why 135

Networking Tactics - What to Talk About and Why 136

Principles of Targeted Networking 138

2 - Use 30-Day Sprints 140

3 - Track Your Progress 143

Notes 148

Module 6 - Assess 151

1 - Is the Job a Good Fit for Me? 152

   1 - Understand the Job Itself 153

   2 - Understand the Job Context 156

   3 - Understand the Market Need 161

   4 - How Good of a Fit is Good Enough? 162

2 - Am I a Good Fit for the Job? 164

   1 - Refresh Your Memory 165

   2 - Prepare 165

   3 - Interview 166

   4 - Manage the Process 168

   Types of Interview Questions 168

3 - Job Definition Questions 171

Notes 176

Module 7 - Negotiate and Close 179

1 - Pre-Negotiation Checklist 181

2 - Negotiation Principles 184

3 - Lessons from the Trenches 188

4 - Further Reading 190

5 - Job Offer Checklist 191

6 - Exercise 193

Notes 194

Introduction

1 - Somehow I Became a Headhunter
2 - Overview
3 - Get the Most Out of This Program
4 - Reflection Questions

Introduction

If you want to find a great job - a job that's a great fit for you - you need to develop the skills to conduct a successful job search. And if you want more out of your career - more impact, more meaning, more learning and growth - finding a great next job is the first step.

Navigating Successful Job Transitions is written for executives and knowledge workers who are looking for, or starting to think about looking for, their next job.

I am going to show you a step-by-step process for conducting a thoughtful, proactive, targeted job search that will help you find a job that's a great fit. But that's just the tip of the iceberg.

I am also going to show you how everything about work and jobs and careers has changed. How stability and certainty have been replaced by constant change and complexity. How traditional career management is seriously flawed. How new school career wisdom "flips the model" and elevates the job search to the foundation of building a successful career. How there are more new and exciting and interesting types of work available today than ever before. How there's never been a better time to learn how do conduct successful job searches and get more from your career.

Let's get started.

1 - Somehow I Became a Headhunter

I never gave much thought to my career. I was the first person in my family to attend college, and my high school didn't provide any college or career guidance. I attended a local college because it was convenient and affordable. My uncle said something about computers being important, so I majored in computer science. I earned an undergrad and then a master's degree. I did well and made good grades, but I was just kind of drifting along, mostly taking cues from others and not making my own decisions. I was fortunate, but not intentional. After completing my Ph.D. coursework, I became disillusioned with the academic world and decided to get a real job.

I spent the next two years in a large corporation working on projects that were either postponed, cancelled, or never materialized. I was bored. A headhunter from another large corporation called me with a job that paid more money, so I took the job. Over the next six years, I got promoted, I got raises, and I bought a condo. But I wasn't having much of an impact, and I wasn't learning and growing.

I decided it was time to do something different, but I wasn't sure what. I considered returning to school to study business, music, or alternative medicine. I spent over a year doing research. I talked to a lot of people. Ultimately, I chose business school. My friends thought I was crazy, but I was pretty excited.

The Legend of David Baldwin

I attended business school at The University of Texas. It was there that I met David Baldwin, a UT business school alum. Like me, David returned to business school to do something different. Unlike me, David had a plan.

During his first year of business school, David talked to several of his classmates to better understand their jobs and careers prior to business school. Based on these discussions, he picked a career direction, made a list of companies in the field, and then started networking his way into those companies. Not only did David find a great job, but he is still working with the same company today.

David spoke to one of my business school classes and shared his job search process. He talked about informational interviewing. He talked about networking beyond your existing network. He talked about not limiting yourself to the small number of companies that recruited on campus. His last idea really struck me! You mean you could get a job with a company that didn't recruit on campus? Of course, I completely ignored David's ideas and advice. Everyone else was strolling down to the career services office to sign up for interviews, so I strolled as well. Without giving a lot of thought to what I really wanted to do with my career, I accepted a job with McKinsey & Company and moved to Dallas.

To be clear, McKinsey was a great experience and a highly regarded company, but I didn't make a conscious decision to do consulting. I wasn't thoughtful or deliberate or focused or proactive. I didn't pursue any companies that didn't recruit on campus. I didn't follow David's advice. I just went with the flow and followed the herd. Predictably, three years later, I was ready to do something different again.

Perhaps it was time to give David Baldwin's job search process a shot.

I gave some thought to what type of job I wanted and where I wanted to live. I decided I wanted to move back to Austin and work for a high-tech startup in a product marketing role. I put together a list of people and companies in Austin and started networking. I did a lot of informational interviews, asking questions rather than looking for a job. This turned out to be more important than I would have imagined (more on this soon).

I spent the next four months pursuing product marketing jobs in Austin. As I learned more about these jobs, I validated their fit with my experience. The market seemed to validate the fit as well. I did some product marketing consulting on the side, which gave me cash to extend my search and also provided real hands-on experience. I received a handful of offers for product marketing roles for high-tech startups in Austin.

But I wasn't very excited about the offers.

The roles just didn't seem that impactful, and the products these companies were building weren't that exciting (at least to me). And the people didn't seem engaged. I remember spending a Friday at one of the companies, watching people leave the office in the middle of the afternoon. At 4:30pm, I was the only person left, and I wasn't even an employee. I wanted to work with people who were fired up.

I ended up turning down all of the offers.

But about the same time, a new type of opportunity started to emerge. Actually, it had been hovering in the background all along, but I hadn't noticed.

While conducting informational interviews, I had asked people (mostly entrepreneurs, startup executives, and investors) how they spent their time and what were their biggest problems. I heard things like, "My biggest challenge is recruiting people to grow our company." Or, "I spend way too much time on recruiting." Or, "Recruiting is a big challenge for us, and none of the recruiters we've used are very good." Initially, it didn't sink in. I was focused on product marketing roles. I ignored the feedback. But as my excitement for product marketing roles waned, I began to pay more attention. This sounded like an interesting problem to try to solve.

So I began researching the recruiting industry. I talked to recruiters. I talked to startup executives. I talked to more recruiters. The idea started to become real. A couple of the recruiters said they thought I might make a good recruiter. The momentum increased. And then suddenly the interesting problem I was researching resulted in a job offer to become a recruiter.

I talked to a few mentors. They asked good questions about recruiting, some of which I could not answer. I didn't have a clear grasp of what it meant to be a recruiter, what the job entailed on a daily basis, what skills were important, and what defined success.

I arranged to spend two days shadowing an experienced senior recruiter to see what she did and how she did it. I literally followed her around the office for two days from 8am to 5pm. We got a "Y jack" for her phone, so I could listen in on her phone calls. I asked a lot of questions. The job became more "real", and I gained a much better sense of what recruiting would be like on a day-to-day basis.

Recruiting (specifically recruiting for high-tech startups in Austin, TX) appealed to me on several dimensions.

- **It was a big problem.** In fact, it was one of the biggest problems virtually every high-tech executive and investor was trying to solve.

- **Other recruiters were ignoring the problem.** I talked to a lot of recruiters, none of whom were interested in working with startups. They said startups didn't have any money to pay recruiter fees.
- **I saw an opportunity for a disruptive business model.** Maybe startups didn't have a lot of cash, but they had equity. What if I took part of my fees in cash and part in equity? I could build a diversified portfolio of equity positions in private companies and impact the outcome by recruiting key executives.
- **It kept me close to high-tech startups.** I still had a strong interest in high-tech startups, just not in the specific startups that offered me product marketing jobs.
- **It provided me the opportunity to build my own business within a larger firm.** If I did well, I saw the opportunity to build my own client base, providing me with more autonomy, control, and flexibility.

So I became a headhunter. My friends thought I was crazy, but I was pretty excited. And for the first time in my career, I was intentional and deliberate about the job search process and decision.

There's one additional point worth making. Although I was intentional and deliberate about my search, I did not start out knowing that I wanted to be a recruiter. I followed a process, and the process led me to a great job.

Can You Help Me Find a Job?

It was 1998, and I had a new job and a new career. The Internet was taking off, and my phone was ringing off the hook. Not with calls from prospective clients, but from people looking for jobs. I tried to be helpful. I asked them what type of job they were looking for. I asked them what they wanted from their career. I asked them if they could work for any company in any position, what company and position would it be. Would they prefer a big company or a startup? Fast growth or slow growth? Innovative or mature? What industries were of interest? What vertical markets? Any particular products or technologies? I asked them to describe their approach to finding their next job. I didn't get many good answers. People knew they wanted something different, but they struggled to articulate it.

I told people about the job search process I learned in business school and how it had worked for me during my own job search. I developed a set of slides that outlined the process, and I shared the slides with anyone who was interested (and a few who weren't). Some people used the process to find a job and shared their experiences with me. I used their feedback to refine the process. A few commented that following the process was transformative.

One day I had lunch with an experienced executive, and he offered to pay me a lot of money to help him find a job. I was caught off guard. This executive didn't need to work, and he didn't need my help to find a job. But he wasn't looking for "just a job". He was looking for work that was interesting and meaningful and a good cultural fit.

I wondered if there were others in the same boat: people who had already enjoyed some degree of success, but wanted something more out of their next job.

I put back on my research hat and started to investigate common job search techniques. I started with the popular literature on job search, career management, and outplacement. Then I reviewed some of the academic literature. I also talked to experts in the industry.

Here's what I discovered:

- Although there is a lot of information out there today, there's also a lot of noise and misinformation (especially on the Internet). Much of the collective wisdom hasn't been updated to reflect the uncertainty, instability, and complexity of today's job market or the vast array of jobs/careers available to most people.

- Most of the popular writings and the academic research have focused on helping unemployed people find a job as fast as possible. Very little has been written on helping people optimize their job search - helping them find a great job as opposed to just any job. People who have had some success and have choices have largely been neglected.

- As a recruiter and a career advisor, I am in the unique position of seeing "both sides of the equation." I've witnessed firsthand how hiring gets done and what influences key decisions, and I've seen how people find great jobs and manage their careers.

- Most executives don't know how to conduct an effective job search. They suboptimize their career transitions by taking a haphazard, passive, and somewhat arbitrary approach. In doing so, they are not getting all they can out of their careers.

- Conducting a successful job search is simple, but it's not necessarily easy. It requires a fair amount of effort. It requires taking responsibility for your career. It requires contemplation as well as action. It's a lot more difficult than staring at a computer monitor, surfing career sites, and applying for jobs online. But it actually works.

Learn How to Fish for Yourself

The world of work has changed radically over the last several years, and it's unlikely we'll ever return to a world characterized by stability and certainty. Although we're faced with new challenges, we're also presented with unprecedented opportunities. Those who get more out of their jobs and careers will take responsibility for managing their careers. They'll invest the time and effort to understand the new world of work, the new mindsets that support it, and the new skills needed to navigate it.

As the old saying goes, "Give a man a fish and you feed him for a day. Teach a man how to fish and you feed him for a lifetime."

> Learn how to consistently navigate successful career transitions, and you'll get more out of the rest of your career.

2 - Overview

If you want more from your career and you're willing to work to get it, then this book is for you. Here's what we'll cover:

- **Module 1 - Rethink.** Old school career management no longer works, and it no longer works because virtually everything about jobs and work and careers has changed. In this Module, we'll introduce ***Agile Career Development***, a new school approach to career management that provides new mindsets, frameworks, processes, and tools that will help guide us in the 21st century. Agile Career Development "flips the model", replacing top-down, long-term career planning with bottom-up, short-term agility, and recognizing that the individual has more options than ever before to craft a meaningful career. In the new world of work, agility is the new stability. You'll learn that the most profound implication of Agile Career Development is the elevation of the job search from something you do once every four years out of necessity to the foundation of effective career management.

- **Module 2 - Review and Reflect.** One tried and true model, inspired by Jim Collins in his best-selling book, Good to Great, suggests that a good job lies at the intersection of your career values (or motivations or interests or passions), your career experience (or knowledge, skills, and abilities), and what the market needs and values. In this Module, you'll review and reflect upon your career, exploring your career values as well as your career experience.

- **Module 3 - Focus.** If you already have a strong sense of what your next job looks like, that's great. You've got your Target Job Profile. If not, we introduce an exploration technique that will allow you to create more focus and clarity around what's next for you. For many of you, this Module will be quite painful, as it will force you to eliminate some options and focus your search.

- **Module 4 - Prepare.** Armed with a strong sense of your next job, you're ready to start building your target list of companies and target list of people, the two most important documents you'll create during your search. You'll also craft a resume and develop an elevator pitch.

- **Module 5 - Execute.** To execute a successful job search, you need to run a process. Investment bankers run a process when they are trying to sell a company because a process generates more buyers, maximizes valuation, and helps find buyers with aligned interests. Executive recruiters run a process when they are trying to fill a key executive position because a process generates more candidates, uncovers the most qualified candidates, and provides the perspective needed to select the best candidate available. People who want more from their careers run a process when they are navigating transitions because a process prepares them well for a successful search, results in more and better opportunities, and provides mechanisms to course correct if needed. The process you'll learn is rigorous, targeted, and proactive. By contrast, most people navigate transitions in a more arbitrary, scattered, and reactive manner. You'll use 30-day sprints to focus your efforts and Weekly Scorecards to track your activity as well as your progress.

- **Module 6 - Assess.** As you execute your search and begin to have conversations with Hiring Managers, you will enter the assessment phase. When you talk to Hiring Managers, two things happen. They assess you, and you assess them. Hiring Managers assess you primarily through interviews and reference checks. You'll assess them through interviews and reference checks as well. To determine whether or not a job is a good fit for you, you'll consider the job itself (the work you'll actually be doing), the job context (how, where, why, and with whom the work gets done), and the job economics (compensation economics and career economics).

- **Module 7 - Negotiate and Close.** When you find a job that's a good fit, you'll negotiate and close the deal. During this phase, there is often lots of excitement, and there can be a temptation to neglect reverse reference checks, shortcut due diligence, and ignore cautionary flags. You'll use the pre-negotiation checklist to prepare before you start to negotiate. After you receive an offer, you'll use the job offer checklist as a guideline while reviewing. You'll also use my negotiation principles and lessons learned to help keep things on track and optimize the chances of a favorable outcome.

3 - Get the Most Out of This Program

In the 1960s, a Stanford professor named Walter Mischel conducted a series of psychological studies, which became known as the Stanford marshmallow experiment. In these studies, a child (usually four or five years old) was offered a choice between one marshmallow provided immediately or two marshmallows if they waited 15 minutes. In follow up studies, the researchers found that children who were able to wait longer for the marshmallows tended to have better life outcomes, as measured by SAT scores, lower levels of substance abuse, lower likelihood of obesity, better responses to stress, better social skills as reported by their parents, and generally better scores in a range of other life measures. Since then, much has been written about the power of delayed gratification.

> If you want to get the most out of this program, not only is it going to take some effort, it's also going to take patience and persistence.

Meet Russell Diez-Canseco, a Harvard MBA, former CIA Officer, former McKinsey Manager, and former corporate Vice President. By almost any standard, Russell has enjoyed a successful career. But when I talked to Russell in late 2013, he was looking for a new job, and he wanted to live and work in Austin, TX. Russell used this program to navigate a successful career transition. I caught up with Russell in October 2014 to talk about his experience. Here's what he said:

> It's important to reflect upon your career and what you think you want to do next before jumping in. Deciding what to do and getting focused was the hardest part: it's frightening to eliminate options. But instead of deciding, I hit my network and got some leads. They didn't pan out, and that shook my confidence. So several months into my search, I decided I needed to restart and do it right. To extend my search and not rush a decision, I did some consulting on the side. I explored the education and food industries, two areas in which I had an interest and at least some experience. I realized that exploring and deciding are an iterative process, but at some point you must force a decision - even if it's artificial. I made a list of education and food companies in Austin and started calling them. One of the companies was Vital Farms, the largest provider of pasture-raised eggs and poultry in the United States. I took a job there and am currently

> their VP of Operations and Supply Chain. I've already made a huge impact, and I couldn't be happier. *Update - Russell was recently promoted to Chief Operating Officer.*

Russell's story is not unusual. He picked up the marshmallow, but then got back on track. And when he did, his effort, patience, and persistence paid off.

Resisting marshmallows is one of six key principles that will help you get the most out of this program and your job transition.

1 - Invest the Time

Research has shown a direct correlation between amount of time invested in a job transition and the results, yet most people spend way too little time on their search. Orville Pierson, a veteran job search expert and author of several career books, reported that unemployed people spend less than 10 hours per week on their job search. That's just not enough. If you're unemployed, conducting a successful job search should be a full-time job. I suggest spending at least 30 hours per week, and you'll probably spend more during the initial 30 days. If you're employed, plan to spend at least 10 hours per week.

2 - Resist the Mighty Marshmallow

Resisting marshmallows means following the process described in this book in the face of opportunities that might fall in your lap. Too many people start following the process with great intentions, but then a couple of weeks into their search, their network starts to ping them with job opportunities. Flush with confidence, they put the process on hold to pursue the marshmallows. After a couple of months, these early opportunities usually lead nowhere or to a job that's less than ideal. Only then do most people recommit and follow the process. To be clear, it's possible that the perfect job may fall in your lap early on. But it's very unlikely, and even if it does, you may not recognize it. Nibble on the marshmallows if you must, but just don't stop the process.

3 - Give Yourself Enough Runway

Not only is it important to invest enough time (on a weekly basis) and resist the marshmallows, but it's also important to give yourself enough runway. Your runway is the amount of time you have before your job search becomes economically painful. I suggest giving yourself 6 months if you're unemployed and working on your search at least 30 hours per week and at least 12 months if you're employed and working on your search 10 hours per week. Remember, you're looking for a job that's a great fit for you - you're not just looking for the first job that pops up.

There are two important reasons for giving yourself enough runway:

- First, you need to develop an informed perspective on the job market, and this takes time. Without perspective, it's difficult to determine whether a job opportunity that presents itself is an awesome opportunity or just an average opportunity.

- Second, you want to be in the market long enough to expose yourself to a large enough set of interesting opportunities.

Russell Diez-Canseco extended his runway by doing consulting on the side. James Decker (whom you'll meet soon) started his search while employed full-time, and then after gaining market perspective and confidence, quit his job to work on his search full-time.

4 - Manage the Ups and Downs

In his best-selling book, Guerrilla Tactics in the Job Market, Tom Jackson characterized a typical job search as "no, no, no, no, no, no, no, no, no, no, no, no, no, no, no, no, no, no, no, no, no, no, yes." That's a lot of rejection, even for the most confident and successful executives. In fact, it is often the most successful executives who struggle the most with rejection. Just remember - it's basically a numbers game. Have faith in the process, and look to others for advice and support.

5 - Keep Score

One of the best ways to manage the ups and downs is to keep score. Keeping score means tracking your *activity* and your *progress*. Tracking your activity allows you to gain a clear picture of whether or not you're investing sufficient time and energy on your search. Tracking *progress* involves a set of metrics related directly to the process you'll learn about in this book. People who can see their progress are less likely to abandon the process prematurely. You'll use Weekly Scorecards during this program to track your activity and progress.

6 - Enlist the Support of Others

Working with others on a career transition has been shown to lead to higher success rates and shortened duration, and a study conducted in 2009 by Christopher Kondo noted the following qualitative benefits as well:

- improved understanding of the job search process
- social and emotional support
- accountability
- gratification from helping others
- exposure to job and networking leads

The Kondo study highlighted another key difference between those working in groups and those working alone. Those working in groups spent 25-40 hours per week and were generally satisfied with their job search. By contrast, those working alone spent 10-15 hours per week and were more likely to feel mistreated by previous employers, blame job search difficulties on external factors, and feel frustrated with the job search process.

4 - Reflection Questions

1. What are your primary motivations for wanting to make a transition? Check all that apply.

    - I'm underpaid.
    - I have an irritating boss.
    - I work in a toxic company culture.
    - The actual work is boring.
    - The actual work is too demanding.
    - I want a job that provides an opportunity for more learning and growth.
    - I want a job that makes more of an impact.
    - I want a job that has more meaning.
    - I want to travel less.
    - I want more balance in my life.
    - I'm currently unemployed and need work.
    - Other (please list).

2. How have you found jobs in the past?

3. Are there any specific companies that interest you? Why?

4. Are there any specific industries that interest you? Why?

5. Are there any specific products or technologies that interest you? Why?

6. How many hours per week will you be able to invest in your job search?

7. How much runway do you have?

8. If you are unemployed and have less than 6 months of runway, how do you plan to extend it?

Notes

Module 1 - Rethink

1 - Rethink Career Management
2 - Rethink the Job Search
3 - Reflection Questions

Module 1 - Rethink

It's important to understand the changes that have taken place and the new paradigms that have emerged before covering the tactics of navigating a job transition.

In this Module, you'll see that old school career management no longer works, and it no longer works because virtually everything about jobs and work and careers has changed. **Agile Career Development** is a new school approach to career management that provides new mindsets, frameworks, processes, and tools that will help guide us in the 21st century. Agile Career Development "flips the model", replacing top-down, long-term career planning with bottom-up, short-term agility, and recognizing that the individual has more options than ever before to craft a meaningful career. In the new world of work, *agility is the new stability*.

The most profound implication of Agile Career Development is the elevation of the job search from something you do once every four years out of necessity to the foundation of effective career management.

The job search itself is widely misunderstood. Networking is the way that most people find jobs, and it's the way people find the best jobs. Not through online job sites. Not through recruiters. Not through social media. Not through executive job clubs. But effective networking is not just asking your friends and colleagues if they know of any good jobs. It requires developing connections outside of your existing network. It requires connecting with Hiring Managers and influencers before a job is broadly socialized. Once a job is posted or given to a recruiter, your odds of success are infinitesimally small. To help you network effectively, we'll introduce **Targeted Networking**, a technique that aligns your job search with the way that Hiring Managers fill jobs.

"Our institutions are out of date; the long career is dead; any quest for solid rules is pointless, since we will be constantly rethinking them; you can't rely on an established business model or a corporate ladder to point your way; silos between industries are breaking down; anything settled is vulnerable. Put this way, the chaos ahead sounds pretty grim. But its corollary is profound: This is the moment for an explosion of opportunity, there for the taking by those prepared to embrace the change.

To flourish requires a new kind of openness. More than 150 years ago, Charles Darwin foreshadowed this era in his description of natural selection: "It is not the strongest of the species that survives; nor the most intelligent that survives. It is the one that is most adaptable to change." As we traverse this treacherous, exciting bridge to tomorrow, there is no clearer message than that."

This is Generation Flux *by Robert Safian*
Editor and Managing Director, Fast Company

1 - Rethink Career Management

If you want more out of your work and career, apparently you're not alone.

According to a survey by job-placement firm Manpower, 84% of employed workers planned to look for a new position. One Gallup survey indicated only 20% of all people really like what they do each day, and another Gallup survey indicated 71% of American workers are "not engaged" or "actively disengaged" in their work. Mercer's recent comprehensive report entitled Inside Employees' Minds, begins with the following statement: *Mercer research confirms: Employees are not happy*. My own experience as a recruiter reflects the same malaise.

Yet, few of us are adept at effectively managing our careers and consistently finding the work we desire.

It's illuminating to understand why.

Contemporary career management evolved during the period beginning roughly at the end of WW II and lasting until the 1980s, an era characterized by relative career stability and predictability. During this period, the recipe for successful career management went something like this:

- **Step 1.** Start with introspection and self-reflection to identify your passions (what's your calling?).
- **Step 2.** Understand your traits and abilities (what are you really good at?).
- **Step 3.** Consider possible career options in light of your passions and abilities.
- **Step 4.** Mix everything together, shake vigorously, and voila! Your ideal career is in finance (or sales or as an attorney or a nuclear physicist).
- **Step 5.** Build your long-term career plan (where do you want to be in 30 years?), and then work backwards to set well-defined intermediate goals.
- **Step 6.** Get an entry-level job in your chosen field, and work your way up the corporate ladder.

Sound familiar? It should - it's probably what you were taught, if you were taught anything. The problem is it no longer works (some would argue it never really worked that well to begin with), and it no longer works because virtually everything about jobs and work and careers has changed. **Why we work, where we work, how we work, what work we do, who we work with, when we work - it's all changed.** And just like the boiling frog, we may not fully appreciate the magnitude of the change even though we're completely immersed in it. Conventional career management advice, still prevalent today, is based on a set of outdated and fundamentally flawed assumptions.

- **Flawed assumption 1: The job market is stable and predictable.** Long-term career planning works best in a stable, predictable environment, and today's job market is anything but stable and predictable. Things are changing too quickly. Technology and globalization have created a hyperconnected world where change propagates faster than ever. The Great Recession, which was the worst recession since World War II, struck quickly and was more global than prior recessions. Stability and predictability have been replaced by uncertainty and change, making it increasingly difficult to plan far into the future.

- **Flawed assumption 2: We are aware of all possible job and career options.** There are more job and career choices today than ever, and it's impossible to understand all of the options. Busy executives have their heads down working hard, and they invest little time developing their career awareness. In addition, there are important nuances within careers and jobs that are often overlooked. Some careers in sales may require strong interpersonal skills and high energy while others may require thoughtful analysis and planning. There are also new jobs and careers that require unique and novel combinations of skills and experiences.

- **Flawed assumption 3: Through introspection, we can understand ourselves, our abilities, and our passions.** Peter Drucker once said, "Most people think they know what they are good at. They are usually wrong." Truly understanding our abilities and passions doesn't happen overnight. More typically, abilities and passions are revealed through experience during the course of our careers. Sometimes people have abilities that lie dormant for a long time. Other times unique combinations of abilities are enabled and realized through new markets and new types of jobs. Passions often start as interests that are nurtured and eventually lead to meaningful and impactful work. Passion is usually not something that emerges from introspection.

Career management needs an ***extreme makeover***, one that provides new mindsets, frameworks, processes, and tools that will help guide us in the 21st century. One that leverages principles that embrace complexity, uncertainty, constant change, and imperfect information. One that recognizes that there are more interesting opportunities available than ever before.

Agility is the New Stability

Many, many years before I became an executive recruiter and career advisor, I developed software and studied computer science. When I started my career as a software developer, software was created using the waterfall methodology. Developers would define the product, and then go off and build it. Or at least they'd try. Some products would take months or even years to develop. When the product was finally completed and released (many were scrapped prior to completion), the product seldom met users' expectations. Over time, software developers began to use agile software development methodologies based on iterative and incremental development. They got feedback from users during the development process and used the feedback to develop a more useful product. Agile development was much more effective than the waterfall method for dealing with complexity, uncertainty, and change. Today, some agile software developers release new versions of their products every day. The cycle has been compressed from years to days, and the result has been better products.

Agility is often an effective antidote for complexity, uncertainty, and change, and for knowledge workers in the 21st century, an agile approach to career management is often more effective than conventional old school career wisdom. And since my new school approach to career management shares much with the philosophy behind Agile Software Development, I refer to it as ***Agile Career Development***.

Agile Career Development includes four guiding principles:

1 - Replace Long-Term Planning with Short-Term Iterations.

Things change too quickly to plan too far in advance. Instead of developing a 30-year career plan, focus on optimizing your next job search. String together a series of successful jobs, and your career will take care of itself. Even if you choose to search for a next job that's substantively the same as you current job, it's useful to consider alternatives during each job transition. Heed the advice Facebook COO Sheryl Sandberg offered the graduating class of Harvard Business School in May 2013: *Don't plan too much, and don't expect a direct climb. If I had mapped out my career when I was sitting where you are, I would have missed my career.*

- Note 1. Long-term planning and short-term planning are endpoints on the continuum of career planning. I suggest staying closer to the short-term planning end of the spectrum. If you feel more comfortable with a long-term career plan, fine, but make sure to re-evaluate it annually.

- Note 2. Consider letting your career values (more on this soon) provide direction and guidance throughout your career instead of a long-term career plan.

2 - Get Out of the Office and Collect Real Data.

Instead of relying only on intuition, introspection, and reflection, get out of the office and collect some real data. Reflection is often a good starting point, but it only takes you so far. Action creates clarity, and effective career management mandates that you make a habit of getting out of the office, talking to people, and building relationships. Develop your own sense of what's going on in the market. Some of the hottest companies, fastest-growing industries, and most disruptive innovations may not have existed the last time you looked for a job. Understand how the market values your skills and abilities. Learn how to get real market data to test hypotheses before making important career decisions.

3 - Expect the Unexpected.

If you're getting out of the office and talking to people, you'll become aware of opportunities you hadn't thought of and opportunities you didn't know existed. Many will lead to dead ends, but a few will be worth investigating. I must have heard CEOs and entrepreneurs tell me that recruiting was one of their biggest problems 20 times before it hit me: this could be an interesting opportunity.

4 - Look for Creative Ways to Leverage Your Experience.

Look for opportunities to leverage what you know and who you know - your experience, skills, abilities, and network - in adjacent areas. The adjacent possible, a term taken from Cal Newport who took it from Steven Johnson who took it from Stuart Kauffman, refers to the adjacent space that contains the possible new combinations of existing ideas. At first I thought recruiting was a 180 degrees from my experience, but upon further research, I realized it was really a close adjacency, or pivot, as author and career coach Jenny Blake would call it. Recruiting leveraged my background in computer science and technology, my experience as a consultant, and my network (many people in my network were prospective clients).

Embrace the Lowly Job Search

The old school, top-down, long-term planning approach to career management works best in a stable, predictable world with limited options. Today, effective career management is less about picking the one right career for you and more about conducting successful job transitions. This new school, bottom-up, short-term approach is much better suited to today's rapidly changing world with increasing job and career opportunities.

> Perhaps the most profound implication of a new school approach to career management is the elevation of the job search from something you do once every four years out of necessity to the foundation of effective career management.

This merits repeating.

The lowly job search - that thing that you avoid until you can no longer avoid it, that thing that annoys you, that thing that makes you feel uncomfortable - has become one of the most important career skills you can master in the 21st century.

If the poor, lowly job search is now so important, perhaps we should consider it in more detail.

2 - Rethink the Job Search

New school career management elevates the importance of conducting a job search from **something you do once every four years out of necessity** to the **foundation of effective career management**.

Which begs the question, what's the best way to conduct a job search?

What process should you use? Where should you begin? Should you update your resume and send it to recruiters? Should you contact your network to see if they know of any good jobs? Should you troll the online job sites? Should you join one of the "exclusive" job clubs that claim access to the hidden job market? And what about social media? Isn't everyone finding jobs on social media these days?

During my nearly 20 years of helping people find jobs and recruiting executives, I've come across very few people who consistently conduct effective job searches. If you're a bit unsure of the best way to conduct a job search yourself, there's a good reason.

No One Taught You How

Job search techniques are not taught in most schools. In fact, it's worse than that. Most leading university career services offices attract large companies to campus to recruit graduating students, alleviating the need for students to learn how to conduct a successful job search. **The university job search experience sets a dangerous precedent in that it gives us the impression that job search is a predominantly passive activity and that good jobs will come to you.** For many students, the job search becomes a "beauty pageant" where they pick the best looking job, and off they go. But, this beauty pageant approach to job search is not reality in today's job market, and it's becoming less of a reality for even the best and brightest in the top colleges.

Job search techniques are typically something people are forced to learn on their own. But a lot of the common knowledge about how to find a job is just not very helpful. Some of it is outdated (like mailing resumes and cover letters), some is well-intended but misses the mark (like poor networking advice), and some is the result of the biased information published by online job sites that have a vested interest in getting people to use their sites to find jobs.

Here's an example. Go to Google and type in "job search." What pops up? Online job sites. A gazillion of them. Is this because online jobs sites are the best way to find a job? Or, is it because many online job sites invest in organic and paid search techniques that garner high page rankings on Google and other search engines? Spend some time trolling the online job sites, and it's likely you'll come away thinking that the easiest way to find a great job is online. Just post your resume, and employers will find *you*. Or search from tens of thousands of awesome jobs, and pick the one you want. It's just that easy! Except it's not.

Network, Network, Network

If you manage to escape the seduction of the online job sites, you might discover that **80% of all people find jobs through networking** (and the percentage is higher for executives and knowledge workers). But networking effectiveness varies widely with approach, and most people don't network very well. They contact their friends and colleagues, and they ask them if they're aware of any opportunities that might be a good fit. Or they tell them they just want to get on their radar in case they hear of anything interesting. If you've ever tried this, you know it's not very effective. Effective networking is one of the key tactics we'll cover in detail in this book, but for now keep in mind these two points:

- To network effectively, we need to connect with people we don't already know.
- To network effectively, we need to stop focusing on open jobs.

The Strength of Weak Ties

In the late 1960s, Mark Granovetter, a PhD student at Harvard, decided to try to figure out how people find jobs. His research confirmed what we already know - that most people find jobs through networking (Granovetter's research and the research of others he cites put the percentage between 60% and 90%). Interestingly, not only did most people find jobs through networking, but **networking led to the highest-quality jobs, the most satisfying jobs, and the jobs in which people stayed the longest**.

But Granovetter's research also dispelled a commonly held belief - that our circle of close friends and colleagues (strong ties) provide more value during a job search than people we hardly know (weak ties). Put another way, *if we focus our networking*

efforts on our existing network of contacts (our strong ties), we're severely limiting the amount of information and the number and quality of job opportunities to which we're exposed.

Since Granovetter published his original paper, The Strength of Weak Ties, in 1973, additional research has been conducted to better understand why your close friends and colleagues (strong ties) are less helpful to you than casual acquaintances (weak ties). It turns out that people generally don't refer their close friends to jobs for two reasons:

- they are more worried that it will reflect badly on them if things don't work out,
- they are more likely to know of the faults of their close friends and believe these could interfere with being a good worker.

There's nothing wrong with initial networking with friends and colleagues. It's a great place to start, and it might lead to some low-hanging fruit. But it's only the tip of the iceberg. David Baldwin told me his most valuable contacts during his job search were 4-5 connections from his current network. My own experience is consistent with David's. To conduct a successful job search, we need to expand our network. We need to reach beyond our comfort zone.

And we also need to better align our networking efforts with the way most people get hired.

Job Search Alignment

Let's put ourselves in the shoes of an executive who needs to fill a job. Let's call that person the Hiring Manager. He/she could be a CEO, a Vice President, or other executive/manager. But it's *not* someone from Human Resources. It's the person to whom the job reports.

From the Hiring Manager's point of view, many mid-level and executive positions follow some variation of the following process.

- **Phase 1 - Formulation**. The Hiring Manager starts to formulate the need for a position. Perhaps the current person in a job is not performing well, or perhaps there is a need for a new position. Importantly, as she talks to people and meets with people during this phase, she may be considering their fit for the job (although she may not disclose this). People who meet with Hiring Managers during this phase may actually be interviewing for a job they don't know exists.

- **Phase 2 - Narrow socialization**. The Hiring Manager has formulated the need and now has a job to fill. She puts together a short list of candidates (perhaps an internal candidate, someone she knows well, or someone she has met during the formulation phase), and then she taps her network as well as the network of a few colleagues or trusted advisors to see if anyone knows of any good candidates. There's a candidate pool, but it's small compared to the hundreds of candidates you might see from a posted position, and it's created from a small network of people close to the Hiring Manager (let's call these people Influencers). At this point, the position has been *narrowly socialized*, but it hasn't been posted, given to a recruiter, or broadly socialized. Roughly 80% of jobs are filled during this phase. Not only are *most* jobs filled during this phase, but the *best* jobs are filled during this phase (another Granovetter discovery). And it's the way that the top companies and most experienced Hiring Managers fill their key positions. In his bestselling book, Who - The A Method for Hiring, Geoff Smart devotes an entire chapter to sourcing candidates and generating a flow of "A players." According to Smart, "Of all the ways to source candidates, the number one method is to ask for referrals from your personal and professional networks."

- **Phase 3 - Broad socialization**. If the limited candidate pool approach doesn't work, the Hiring Manager may consider socializing the position more broadly and creating a much bigger candidate pool - either by posting (for less important roles) or by using a recruiter (for more important roles). The remaining 20% of jobs that were not filled during the prior phase are filled during this phase.

The Sweet Spot

Let's take a closer look at the example above and run some numbers. We'll make some simplifying assumptions, but the point should still be clear.

Here's the setup:

- You're looking for a sales leadership role in a technology company. In a smaller company (25M - 100M), this might be a VP Sales role. In a larger company (100M - 1B), it might be a Sales Director and Sales Manager role.
- Based on some research, you discover there are 40 such positions within your area of geographic focus. You also discover, much to your dismay, that all 40 of these positions are currently filled.
- You also know that people change jobs on average every four years, so we can expect 10 of the 40 positions to turn over in the next 12 months. Now you're a bit more encouraged. You'll just sit back and wait until those 10 jobs open up, and then you'll check them out.
- But then you realize that 8 of those 10 jobs will never "open up". They'll be filled through a limited candidate pool and never be broadly socialized.

If only 20% of these jobs are ever posted or given to a recruiter, then you should focus only about 20% of your time on these jobs. Makes sense, right? In fact, that's exactly what conventional career wisdom suggests.

Not so fast.

The 80% of jobs filled through limited socialization have fewer candidates than the 20% of jobs filled through broad socialization. ***So your odds are different.*** Let's say the 80% of jobs filled through limited socialization have 20 candidates each whereas the 20% filled through broad socialization have 100 candidates each (probably a gross underestimate). Your odds are 1 in 20 for one of the 8 narrowly socialized jobs and 1 in 100 for one of the 2 broadly socialized jobs. Using simple probability (and assuming your chances are the same as all other candidates), your chances of getting one of the narrowly socialized jobs is 34%, and your chances of getting one of the broadly socialized jobs is 2%.

In other words, ***you have a 17 times greater chance of getting one of those ten sales jobs if you find out about it before it's posted or given to a recruiter.*** Why spend even 20% of your time on jobs that you have almost no chance of getting when you can get much better odds elsewhere? Focus your efforts on "the sweet spot", not on positions that are broadly socialized (see Figure 2).

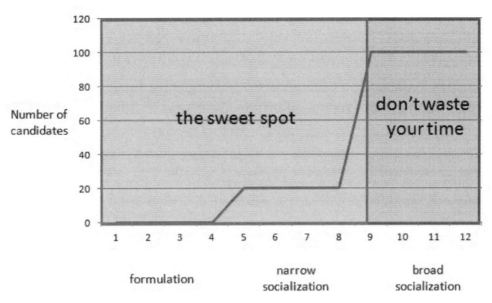

Figure 2 - The sweet spot

Do You Know of Any Good Jobs?

Let's review what we've learned so far:

- Networking is the way that most people find jobs, and it's the way most people find the best jobs. Not through online job sites. Not through recruiters. Not through social media. Not through executive job clubs.
- Networking is not just asking your friends and colleagues if they know of any good jobs. It requires developing connections outside of your existing network.
- Networking requires connecting with Hiring Managers and Influencers before the job is broadly socialized. Once a job is posted or given to a recruiter, your odds of success are infinitesimally small.

When you contact your friends and colleagues and ask them if they're aware of any good jobs, you're taking a *job-centric* approach to networking, and you're leveraging your *existing network*. This "know of any good jobs" approach to networking is shown in the lower left quadrant of Figure 3 below.

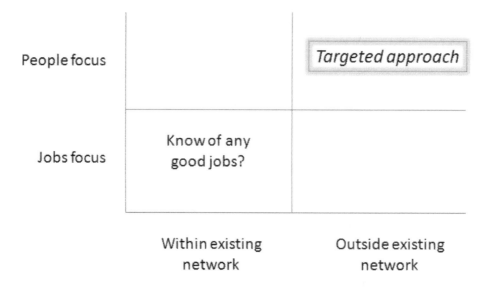

Figure 3 - Targeted job search

By contrast, the approach I advocate is shown in the upper right quadrant. It involves networking **outside of your existing network** (to increase your chances of connecting with Hiring Managers and Influencers, and to minimize any possible strong ties bias), and it involves taking a **people-centric** approach (focusing on networking with Hiring Managers and Influencers instead of networking to find broadly socialized jobs).

Networking outside of your network and **not** looking for jobs (that are broadly socialized) may seem counterintuitive at first. For some, it's uncomfortable - perhaps even unnerving. But it's the key to conducting a successful job search. And if you've ever been in the position of being a Hiring Manager yourself, you know it's really hard to find good people. The opportunity for a Hiring Manager to connect with prospective candidates before he/she is forced to broadly socialize a job (and spend money for a recruiter or posting) is usually welcomed.

Here's a real and recent example of how this works:

> Kevin had been the President of a small division for a mid-sized manufacturing company for just over five years. He turned around his division and improved operational metrics across the board. But there was no upward mobility (his boss was the founder), and his division had little growth potential. Kevin decided it was time to move on.

> A couple of months into his search, Kevin heard about a mid-sized manufacturing company that was moving its headquarters from the west coast to his area. Through online research, he was able to find the name of a potential Hiring Manager within the company in his area. Kevin did not know the Hiring Manager, but he knew someone who knew a potential Influencer (someone who worked for the Hiring Manager). Kevin got a warm introduction to the Influencer and scheduled a phone call with the Influencer. This led to a face-to-face meeting with the Influencer and an introduction to the Hiring Manager.
>
> When Kevin met with the Hiring Manager, he found out about several positions the company was trying to fill, but had not yet posted (the positions were being narrowly socialized). Over the course of the ensuing weeks, Kevin spent more time with the Hiring Manager (and other managers at the company) and was ultimately offered a senior operations position.
>
> But then something unexpected happened.
>
> Kevin had been introduced to the President of another mid-sized manufacturing company who was starting to think about replacing the local General Manager (he was still in the formulation phase). As such, there were no other candidates yet for that position. The company moved quickly with Kevin, offered him the job, and Kevin accepted the General Manager position.

To conduct an effective job search, you need to extend your network, and you need to find out about opportunities before they turn into posted job openings.

3 - Reflection Questions

1. Do you have a long-term career plan? If so, are you following it? How useful has it been? Do you update it every year?

2. Talk to someone you know who has a successful, rewarding career. Ask him/her if his/her success was more the result of long-term career planning or more related to short-term agility (taking advantage of unplanned opportunities).

3. How have you found your last three jobs? Did you find any of them through a recruiter? Through an online job posting? Through an executive job club?

4. How comfortable will you be networking outside of your existing network? What challenges do you anticipate?

5. If your friend, John, introduced you to his friend, Mary, who wanted to speak to you for 15 minutes about your job and your company, would you be willing to have the conversation? Why or why not?

Notes

Module 2 - Review & Reflect

1 - Where Have You Been?
2 - The Career Inventory Exercise
3 - Capture Your Values
4 - The Career Success Exercise
5 - Career Success Worksheet
6 - Capture Your Experience
7 - The Career Experience Exercise
8 - Career Experience Worksheet
9 - Career Experience Example
10 - Capture Your Market Value
11 - Compensation History Exercise
12 - Compensation History Worksheet

Module 2 - Review and Reflect

We covered a lot in Module 1, but it's important to understand the changes that have taken place and the new paradigms that have emerged before covering the tactics of navigating a job transition.

In this Module, we're going to introduce the 3-circle framework, which we'll use throughout the rest of the book. The 3-circle framework is based on the Hedgehog Concept in Jim Collins' best-selling book, Good to Great, and suggests that a good job lies at the intersection of:

- Your career values (or motivations or interests or passions)
- Your career experience (or knowledge, skills, and abilities)
- What the market needs and values

Figure 1 - The 3-Circle Framework

The 3-circle framework is a powerful tool for thinking through and fleshing out what a good job means to you. In this book, you'll use it to describe the type of job you're looking for next; what we call your **Target Job**. Before you launch your job search, you need to develop a strong sense of your Target Job by completing a **Target Job Profile**. Here's an example.

Target Job Profile

Target Position

Industry	software
Industry Segment	analytics software
Function	marketing
Function Segment	product marketing
Vertical Orientation	NA
Size/scale	$25M - $100M
Growth Rate	25% - 100%
Total Staff	1 - 10
Levels Above	1 or 2
Levels Below	1 or 2

Location(s)

Primary	Austin, TX
Secondary	NA

Compensation

Minimum	180K base
Goal	220K base

Market Size Estimates

25 - 35 companies

35 - 50 jobs

Career Values

great product that makes a difference

long-term focus

job autonomy, no micromanging

opportunity for learning and growth

less than 20% travel

work from home 2 days per week

3 weeks vacation

non-execs empowered to make decisions

Example Titles

Chief Marketing Officer (CMO)

Vice President Marketing

Vice President Product Marketing

Example Target Companies

ABC Analytics

DataSoft

XYZ Software and Systems

A few of you may already have a strong enough sense of your next job to complete a Target Job Profile now. But most of you won't.

> **The purpose of this Module and the next Module is to provide you with a step-by-step process for developing your own Target Job Profile before you launch your job search.**

In this Module, you'll review your career to date and reflect on your *career values* (upper left circle), your *career experience* (upper right circle), and your *market value* (lower circle).

1 - Where Have You Been?

In order to develop a sense of where you want to go next (i.e., your next job), it's useful to take a step back and reflect upon where you've been. Doing so often creates a heightened awareness of underlying *career values* (the upper left circle in the 3-circle framework) as well as *career experience* (the upper right circle).

You'll reflect upon where you've been using the Career Inventory Exercise, a series of questions for "interviewing" yourself using a chronological in-depth structured interview process (similar to the [Topgrading](#) system developed by Dr. Brad Smart).

In addition to helping you clarify career values and career experience, completing the Career Inventory Exercise is a prerequisite to updating your resume and preparing for interviews.

2 - The Career Inventory Exercise

The Career Inventory Exercise includes questions about your professional experience as well as your non-professional experience. I believe there is value in thinking beyond your professional experience and including other experience (educational experience, hobbies, volunteer experience, etc.) when contemplating career decisions. Looking beyond traditional career experiences is often a catalyst for better integrating non-professional experience into our careers. For example, Kathy studied writing in college and wrote non-professionally after college, but her current job involved little writing. She didn't want to become a professional writer per se, but she hoped to find a job that included a substantive writing component.

In completing the Career Inventory Exercise, some people have written over 30 pages. Others have written 2 pages. Do what works for you. Virtually everyone who has completed the exercise has found it valuable.

Professional Experience

Answer the following questions for each job you've held. Start with your first job, and proceed in chronological order. If you've had multiple jobs within the same company, it's best to answer the questions for each job.

1) Name of company?
2) Industry?
3) Size of company (revenue and headcount)?
4) Name of business unit (if applicable)?
5) Size of business unit (revenue and headcount)?
6) Your title?
7) To whom did you report (name and title)?
8) How many direct reports did you have?
9) How many total staff did you have?
10) Start date (month/year)?
11) End date (month/year)?

12) How did you find the job? Through a job posting? Through a recruiter? By networking? Other?

13) Was there a formal job opening, or was a position created for you?
14) Where you actively looking for a job when you took the job?

15) What compelled you to take the job? What was the appeal?
16) What criteria did you consider in making your decision?
17) What people influenced your decision and how?
18) To what extent did the job turn out as you anticipated? In what ways was it as expected? Different?

19) What were the three most important things you accomplished in this job?
20) What parts of the job did you enjoy most?
21) What parts of the job did you enjoy least?
22) What were the high points?
23) What were the low points?
24) What were you most proud of?
25) To what extent did you enjoy the day-to-day aspects of the job? What specifically did you enjoy?
26) To what extent did you learn and grow as a result of the job? Can you provide examples?
27) To what extent did you make an impact? Can you give examples?

28) Based on your formal performance reviews as well as informal feedback from others, how would you characterize your performance?
29) If your boss was contacted as a reference, how would he/she likely describe your strengths, weaknesses, and overall performance?
30) If your peers were contacted as references, how would they likely describe your strengths, weaknesses, and overall performance?
31) If your subordinates were contacted as references, how would they likely describe your strengths, weaknesses, and overall performance?

32) What motivated you to look for a new job?
33) Was it more of a "push" away from your current job (bad boss, toxic culture, etc.) or a "pull" towards a new opportunity (more money, more impact, etc.)?

Educational Experience

Answer the following questions for each college or university attended or each degree obtained.

1) What school did you attend?
2) Why did you pick that school? What criteria did you use to make your decision?
3) What was your major? Why did you pick that major? Did you change majors? If so, from what to what?
4) What degree did you receive and when?
5) Has your career path followed or leveraged your degree?
6) What were your favorite classes?
7) In what extracurricular activities were you involved?
8) Did you focus more time on academics or extracurricular activities?
9) What awards or distinctions did you receive?
10) What stories do you most often tell people when discussing your educational experience at this school?
11) Do you ever think about going back to school? If so, for what reason?

Other Experience

This section is meant to capture anything that's important to you outside of your job. The following questions are only guidelines. Please include anything you believe is relevant.

1) In what non-professional activities are you involved? Include hobbies, volunteer activities, clubs, associations, religious activities, etc.
2) Which of these activities are you most excited about?
3) In which of these activities do you invest the most time? How many hours per week on average?
4) What do you enjoy most about these activities? What's in it for you?
5) What rewards or recognition have you received that you are proud of?

Summary Questions

1) Do you see any trends regarding your motivations to change jobs? If so, what are they?
2) What was your favorite job? What made it so great?
3) Do you see any trends regarding your favorite jobs? If so, what are they?

4) What was your least favorite job? What made it so bad?
5) Do you see any trends regarding your least favorite jobs? If so, what are they?
6) Have you ever considered, or are you considering, trying to incorporate some of non-professional interests into your job or career? If so, which ones and how?

3 - Capture Your Values

Congratulations on completing the Career Inventory Exercise! I am hopeful that it caused you to pause for a moment, step back, and reflect more deeply on your career. In this section, we'll dig into your **career values** (the upper left circle in the 3-circle framework).

Traditional career wisdom suggests that career success means *more* money, *more* responsibility, *more* power, *more* authority, *more* control, and *more* status. Dr. Douglas LaBier, a business psychologist, psychotherapist, writer and the Founder and Director of the Center for Progressive Development, was one of the first to recognize that traditional career wisdom might be flawed. Beginning in the 1970s, LaBier conducted extensive research on careers and motivations, culminating in the publishing of Modern Madness: The Hidden Link Between Work and Emotional Conflict, in 1989. LaBier discovered that the drive for success, and its criteria of money, power, and prestige, exists alongside a parallel, but less visible, drive for increased fulfillment and meaning from work. LaBier noted,

> "I often found that people would want to talk about a gnawing feeling of wanting something more meaningful from their work. They didn't have quite the right language back then to express what that would look like other than feeling a gap between their personal values and the trade-offs they had to make to keep moving up in their careers and companies."

Even today, many people still seek the traditional trappings of success. They pursue jobs and careers that provide more money, more power, more status, and more authority. But there are an increasing number of people who are choosing alternatives. They're developing their own sense of what they want from their careers. In doing so, they're developing their own definition of careers success.

Steve runs sales for a 300M company. He's in his 40s and makes half a million dollars annually. By all traditional measures, Steve is wildly successful and at the pinnacle of his career. Yet Steve is looking for a new job - a job that provides him with a better work-life balance, a boss who doesn't micro-manage, and a chance to "give something back." He is willing to take a 30% cut in salary for the right job.

Alan was just hired as the VP Marketing for a small company. He took a smaller base salary (but he shares in the company's upside through a profit-sharing program) and now has a smaller team, but the company provides work-life balance, a learning-oriented culture, and a mission that he's excited about.

Barbara is an experienced sales executive who has run sales for successful companies. She currently works out of a home office and manages a remote team. She turned down a bigger job with more responsibility that would have required her to commute to an office, spend more time traveling, and spend less time with her family.

People like Steve, Alan, and Barbara are rethinking what they want from their careers. They're creating their own definitions of career success based on rethinking what's important to them. How about you - can you claim the same? If not, then starting to develop a better sense of what career success means to you will provide a compass as you navigate your career.

But where do we begin?

The Paradox of More

Creating your own definition of career success starts with understanding that, somewhat paradoxically, getting *more* out of your career usually involves getting *less* of some things, *more* of some things, *just enough* of some things, and *balance* across other things.

Let me be more specific.

Less is better

Over 50 years ago, Frederick Herzberg conducted scientific research on job satisfaction that was published in The Motivation to Work in 1959. His blinding insight was the discovery that what leads to dissatisfaction at work is *not* the opposite of what leads to satisfaction at work. More specifically, Herzberg found that the things that cause dissatisfaction at work (such as a bad boss, low salary, poor working conditions, security, etc.) are often different than what leads to satisfaction at work (such as the work itself, meaning, learning, achievement, etc.). This means we need to consider sources of job dissatisfaction independently, and we need to try to *minimize* them.

Sources of job dissatisfaction that I encounter frequently (in addition to the sources cited above) include long hours, long commute, low salary, corporate politics, too many meetings, too much bureaucracy, a micromanaging boss, spending cuts, poor management decisions, people, and a toxic culture. I'm sure there are many more.

So why would you or anyone else accept a dissatisfying job?

The answer is pretty simple. **We tend to overlook or ignore the warning signs when someone offers us a job.** We say to ourselves, "My new boss seems like a micromanager, but I'm sure I can work around that. Besides, I'll be getting a 20% salary increase and a big slice of equity." Or we rationalize, "I know the job will require 90% travel, but it'll be worth it. It's the coolest company in town, and I'll get a chance to run a much bigger team. I'll do well, and my career will skyrocket."

Sources of dissatisfaction usually begin as minor irritants. Taken individually and occurring infrequently, they may matter little, but when they persist and worsen over time, they often lead to extreme job dissatisfaction. Like a small pebble in your shoe, the initial discomfort is almost negligible, but over time, it can grow to be quite painful.

Minimizing job dissatisfaction is important, but it seldom leads to a satisfying job. *It just leads to a job that's not dissatisfying*. Job satisfaction is more directly related to a different set of factors.

More is better

Herzberg discovered that the factors that lead to job dissatisfaction are *not* the opposite of the factors that lead to job satisfaction. A great boss, fun people, little travel, and minimal bureaucracy are all very desirable. But, if you want more out of your job or career, they won't get you there.

What are the factors that lead to a great job? What are the factors that are more directly related to a satisfying and fulfilling career? What are the things we should try to get more of?

Daniel Pink is the author of Drive: The Surprising Truth About What Motivates Us. Pink believes, as do I, that knowledge workers in the 21st century are motivated primarily by intrinsic rewards, which provide a sense of satisfaction or fulfillment based on the activity itself (and not on any type of external reward or punishment). The satisfaction you receive from solving a puzzle or playing a musical instrument or being a good parent are examples of intrinsic rewards. Pink's book is based on academic research and a theory of motivation known as Self-Determination Theory.

While there are many intrinsic rewards and motivators that may contribute to job satisfaction, I believe there are three that provide the foundation for job and career success.

1. **The work itself.** Do you like the work you do each day? According to a Gallup survey, only 20% of people do. Sure, they'll be some bad days, and perhaps some of the work is not enjoyable, but most of the time on most of the days you should like the work itself.   Chances are if you truly enjoy the work, you're pretty good at it. People who enjoy the work they do find themselves getting things done and wondering where the day went. People who don't enjoy the work they do end up watching the clock.

2. **Learning and growth.** Challenging jobs will provide you with opportunities for learning, which ultimately lead to personal growth, accomplishment, and mastery. The key is finding the right degree of challenge. Too much challenge can lead to frustration and overwhelm. Not enough challenge can lead to boredom and stagnation. I've experienced both situations and found neither sustainable nor enjoyable.

> *The human individual is equipped to learn and go on learning prodigiously from birth to death, and this is precisely what sets him or her apart from all other known forms of life. Man is a learning animal, and the essence of the species is encoded in that simple term.*
>
> George Leonard

Having a job that you enjoy and do well is great. Having an enjoyable job that challenges you to learn and grow is even better.

A lot of successful people I know are well into their careers and have stopped learning. They're really good at what they do, but they're no longer being challenged (at least not much). Their learning curve has slowed dramatically. They're successful, and they're bored.

For those who want more out of their careers, maximizing learning and growth opportunities is a powerful strategy. If you're a knowledge worker in the 21st century, your value is largely a function of your experience, skills, and abilities. ***Rather than pursuing jobs that maximize your short-term economic capital, look for jobs that maximize your long-term career capital.*** If you invest wisely in yourself, two important things happen. First, the money is likely to take care of itself over time. Second, you'll earn the right to take on and solve bigger, more important problems, leading to more meaning.

3. **Meaning.** Choose jobs that have meaning to you and allow you to impact something you care about. That doesn't mean you need to save the world from poverty or solve global climate change, but what you do should be meaningful to you in some way.

One of the interesting aspects of meaning is that it seems to be largely dispositional. In other words, the meaning you derive from a particular job or career is based on *your* perception of the job, not the job itself. In a 1997 study, Amy Wrzesniewski discovered that most people view their work as either a Job (focus on financial rewards and necessity), a Career (focus on advancement), or a Calling (focus on fulfilling, socially useful work). For a specific type of job, roughly 1/3 of the people studied viewed the job as a Job, 1/3 as a Career, and 1/3 as a Calling. The key learning is to choose jobs that have meaning to *you*, not to someone else. Family values/pressures and cultural beliefs can significantly influence our job and career decisions, especially early in our careers.

> *You can never be successful if you spend your life living someone else's dreams.*
> Richard Shell

To get more out of our careers, we want to try to maximize intrinsic motivations, especially enjoyment, learning, and meaning. In contrast to intrinsic rewards, there are things that we want just enough of, but not too much.

Just enough is better

As we've seen, traditional definitions of career success focus primarily on more money, more responsibility, more power, more authority, and more recognition. These are examples of extrinsic rewards.

Extrinsic rewards are not completely useless. Everyone needs money to live, and extrinsic rewards are sometimes useful for providing short-term motivation. But when it comes to extrinsic rewards, **we want just enough of them**. People who focus too much on extrinsic rewards, typically at the expense of intrinsic rewards, are often left unfulfilled and wanting even more.

Another problem with extrinsic rewards is that people tend to overvalue them when making important career decisions. Not long ago, I had a conversation with a senior marketing executive who was offered a job paying less than his current job. He wanted more money and was prepared to turn down the job. In discussing the opportunity with him, it became apparent that the job offered several non-monetary benefits. First, the job offered the executive a chance to move to a city that he and his wife both enjoyed. Second, the job provided the executive a chance to work with a great executive team - a group of people he knew and respected. Third, the job was a strong fit for his skills and provided him the opportunity to learn more about an industry in which he had a particular interest. After reconsidering the job in light of its non-monetary benefits, the executive decided to accept the offer, and it turned out to be a great decision.

Just to be clear, all else being equal, I'd prefer more money to less money. But it's rarely the case that all else is equal. Make sure you make enough money to meet your needs, but beyond that point, evaluate jobs based on non-monetary criteria.

Balance is key

In the context of career success, balance refers to how we allocate our time, energy, and resources across other (non-career related) aspects of our lives. These areas might include family, health, finances, relationships, community, religion, etc. Balance is often overlooked when developing new definitions of career success. People who want more from their careers are usually pretty ambitious. They've invested significant time and energy in their careers. Suggesting they allocate some of their time to non-career activities is often met with disdain.

As Harvard Professor Clayton Christensen notes, "The danger for high-achieving people is that they'll unconsciously allocate their resources to activities that yield the most immediate, tangible accomplishments. This is often in their careers, as this domain of their life provides the most concrete evidence that they are moving forward."

But there's mounting evidence that too much focus on our careers negatively impacts other aspects of our lives and ultimately our careers as well.

In their bestselling book Wellbeing: The Five Essential Elements, co-authors Tom Rath and Jim Harter point out that career wellbeing must be balanced across other important aspects of ourselves, including social wellbeing, financial wellbeing, physical wellbeing, and community wellbeing. The book is based on a comprehensive global study of people in more than 150 countries. The study showed that only 7% of people are doing well in all five areas. Struggling in any one of the five areas damages our overall wellbeing, including our career wellbeing. The authors also discovered that career wellbeing is the most essential of the five elements. People with career wellbeing are more than twice as likely to be thriving in their lives overall.

A Simple Framework for Career Success

People who want more from their careers often pursue extrinsic rewards (such as money, status, power, recognition, etc.), but are left unfulfilled and wanting even more. Over the last several years, we've learned a lot about what leads to more rewarding jobs and careers. Our framework for career success includes not only extrinsic rewards, but also intrinsic rewards, dissatisfiers, and balance (see Figure 1 below).

How Much	What	Examples
Less	Dissatisfiers	Politics, excessive travel, long hours, bad boss
More	Intrinsic motivations	Work itself, learning/growth, meaning
Just enough	Extrinsic motivations	Money, status, power, control
Balance	Our other selves	Social, health, community, spiritual

Figure 1: Career Success Framework

From a career navigation perspective, everything starts with values and motivations. People who like what they do and have rewarding careers have jobs that are well-aligned with their values and motivations. Developing your own definition of career success is a career-oriented values exercise.

4 - The Career Success Exercise

The Career Success Exercise will help you identify and clarify your career values. It's a particularly useful exercise when encountering inflection points in your career or as part of an annual career review. Career values tend to be contextual and relative, so they may evolve and change over time. For example, it's not uncommon to prioritize extrinsic rewards early in your career and intrinsic rewards and balance later in your career. If you're currently looking for a new job or starting to think about what's next, the Career Success Exercise is a key step in the process.

Use the Career Success Framework below as a guide in answering the questions.

How Much	What	Examples
Less	Dissatisfiers	Politics, excessive travel, long hours, bad boss
More	Intrinsic motivations	Work itself, learning/growth, meaning
Just enough	Extrinsic motivations	Money, status, power, control
Balance	Our other selves	Social, health, community, spiritual

Reflection Questions

Answer the questions below for your current or most recent job.

1) Regarding your current job (or most recent job), what are the primary sources of dissatisfaction? Make a list of at least three but no more than five.
2) Regarding your current job (or most recent job), what are the most important extrinsic rewards? Make a list of at least three but no more than five.
3) Regarding your current job (or most recent job), what are the most important intrinsic rewards? Make a list of at least three but no more than five.
4) Regarding your current job (or most recent job), what are the most important non-career elements that you are trying to balance with your career? Make a list of at least three but no more than five.
5) To what extent did you consider sources of dissatisfaction, extrinsic rewards, intrinsic rewards, and balance in deciding to accept your current job (or most recent job)? What were some of the specific elements you considered, and how did you prioritize them?

Values Identification

Regarding your next job or career, consider the values that are most important to you. Use the values mentioned in the Career Success Framework as a guideline, but feel free to make up your own.

1) List three to five sources of dissatisfaction that you hope to eliminate.
2) List three to five extrinsic rewards that are most important to you.
3) List three to five intrinsic rewards that are most important to you.
4) List three to five non-career elements that you hope to balance.

Values Clarification and Prioritization

Consider all of the values you listed in the Values Identification section above.

1) What are your ten most important values?
2) Now narrow that down by circling the top five from your list of ten.
3) Do you have any values that are absolutely non-negotiable? Are there one or two values that you prioritize much higher than other values?

Extra Credit

1) Schedule coffee, lunch, or a 15-minute phone call with a mentor or someone whose career you admire.
2) Ask them what career values are most important to them.
3) Ask them how their career values have changed over the years.

5 - Career Success Worksheet

1) List three to five sources of dissatisfaction that you hope to eliminate.

   _____

2) List three to five extrinsic rewards that are most important to you.

   _____

3) List three to five intrinsic rewards that are most important to you.

   _____

4) List three to five non-career elements that you hope to balance.

   _____

5) What are your ten most important values?

   _____   _____

   _____   _____

   _____   _____

   _____   _____

   _____   _____

6) Now narrow that down by circling the top five from your list of ten.

7) Do you have any values that are absolutely non-negotiable? Are there one or two values that you prioritize much higher than other values?

   _____

6 - Capture Your Experience

In the last section, you considered your *career values* and completed the Career Success Exercise. In this section, you'll examine your *career experience* and tackle the Career Experience Exercise.

When I'm trying to recruit an executive to fill a key position within a company, the first thing I always consider is *career experience*. We're looking for candidates who have experience doing an identical or a very similar job. To be clear, relevant experience is not the only thing we look for - we also look for non-cognitive skills, cultural fit, history of success, etc. - but experience is virtually always the *first* thing we look for.

> Career experience is almost always the first thing Hiring Managers look for as well, especially for senior positions.

Given the importance of career experience, it's useful to review and capture your own career experience. I've developed a simple Career Experience Framework to discuss relevant experience with my recruiting clients (Hiring Managers). Capturing your career experience using the Career Experience Framework enables you to codify your career experience in a language that Hiring Managers understand.

My Career Experience Framework includes nine dimensions:

1. Industry
2. Function
3. Vertical orientation
4. Size/scale
5. Growth rate
6. Total staff
7. Levels above
8. Levels below
9. Location

Here's a bit more color on each dimension.

1 - Industry. There are a number of industry classification systems, such as SIC and NAICS, with which you may be familiar. I find most of them to be outdated and of limited utility for executives and knowledge workers in the 21st century. Instead, I prefer to use LinkedIn's industries (you can find a list on the LinkedIn Advanced People Search page). When capturing your industry experience, I suggest trying to specify an industry segment as well. For example, Computer Software is an industry, and Finance Software and Business Intelligence Software are industry segments.

2 - Function. The most common high-level functions are:

- Sales
- Marketing
- Product development
- Finance
- Manufacturing
- Legal
- HR
- Operations
- Corporate development
- Services (professional services, consulting services, etc.)

As with industries, it's useful to think about high-level categories as well as segments. An example of segments for the marketing function might be corporate marketing, strategic marketing, product marketing, product management, field marketing, lead generation, retention marketing, and marcom/PR. Many larger companies further subdivide these segments.

3 - Vertical orientation. Vertical orientation is the industry to which you market or sell. For example, if you are the VP Sales for a software company that sells primarily to the financial services industry, your industry is software, and your vertical orientation is financial services. When navigating job and career changes, it's often useful to consider related verticals. In the case of financial services, a related vertical worth considering might be insurance.

4 - Size/Scale. Scale refers to the size of companies for which you've worked. The following categorization usually works well:

- <$5M (annual revenue)
- $5M - $25M
- $25M - $100M
- $100M - $500M
- $500M - $2B
- $2B - $25B
- $25B+

You can also think about size/scale in terms of number of employees. LinkedIn uses the following segmentation:

- 1 - 10
- 11 - 50
- 51 - 200
- 201 - 500
- 501 - 1000
- 1001 - 5000
- 5001 - 10000
- 10000+

5 - Growth Rate. Growth rate refers to the rate of growth of annual revenues. The following categorization usually works well:

- <0
- 0
- 1-10%
- 10% - 25%
- 25% - 100%
- 100%+

6 - Total staff. Total staff is the total number of people who report up to you. It includes your direct reports, their direct reports, all the way down to individual contributors. Do

NOT include indirect reports (e.g., dotted-line reports, cross-functional teams or matrixed teams).

- 0
- 1-10
- 10-50
- 50-250
- 250-1000
- 1000+

7 - Levels above. I define levels above as levels from the CEO. Think of this parameter as a way to standardize titles across companies. For example, in one company a VP might report to the CEO, but in another company a VP might report to an SVP who reports to an EVP who reports to a COO who reports to a President who reports to the CEO. Big difference.

- 0 (CEO)
- 1 (reports to CEO)
- 2
- 3
- 4
- 5+

8 - Levels below. How many levels of staff do you have? Do NOT include cross-functional teams or matrixed organizations.

- 0 (individual contributor)
- 1 (1st line manager)
- 2 (2nd line manager)
- 3+

9 - Location. Location is the city or metro area in which you work or the city or metro area you are targeting for your search.

7 - The Career Experience Exercise

For each job you've held over the past 10 years, capture your experience across all nine dimensions of the Career Experience Framework. You can use the worksheet on the next page and the example on the page after that.

If you believe your earlier career experience is relevant, feel free to capture your experience beyond the past 10 years.

8 - Career Experience Worksheet

	Job 1 (most recent)	Job 2	Job 3	Job 4	Job 5
Industry					
Industry segment					
Function					
Function segment					
Vertical orientation					
Size/scale					
Growth rate					
Total staff					
Levels above					
Levels below					
Location					

9 - Career Experience Example

	Job 1 (most recent)	Job 2	Job 3	Job 4	Job 5
Industry	Software	Software	Software		
Industry segment	Financial software	Financial software	Supply chain software		
Function	Marketing	Marketing	Marketing		
Function segment	Product marketing	product management	product management		
Vertical orientation	State government, education (K-12)	none	none		
Size/scale	100M - 500M	2B - 25B	500M - 2B		
Growth rate	10% - 25%	0% - 10%	0% - 10%		
Total staff	10 - 50	11 - 50	1 - 10		
Levels above	2	4	4		
Levels below	2	1	1		
Location	Dallas, TX	Dallas, TX	San Jose, CA		

10 - Capture Your Market Value

In the last two sections, you considered your **career values** and completed the Career Success Exercise, and you examined your **career experience** and completed the Career Experience Exercise. In this section, you'll address your **market value**.

Many people look to salary and compensation surveys to gauge their market value, but my experience indicates that your market value is more a function of your compensation history. Why? Two reasons. First, I've seen a lot of salary surveys, but I've never seen one that is accurate. There are too many variables that determine salary, and salary surveys don't recognize all the variables. For example, industry, Industry growth rate, company location, size of company, ownership structure, profitability, and annual company growth rate are all variables that influence salary, but I've yet to see a salary survey that breaks out these variables. Second, salaries for a given position have a greater variance that most people realize. I've seen many cases where top performers earn 50% more than average performers for the same role.

The best way to gauge your current market value and prepare for salary negotiations is to make sure you have a solid grasp of your compensation history.

11 - The Compensation History Exercise

For each job you've held over the past 10 years, capture your compensation using the worksheet on the next page. Include your starting compensation as well as your ending compensation.

If your compensation history is fairly linear, 10 years of compensation history is sufficient. If you've had higher-paying jobs in the past, it's usually a good idea to include those as well.

12 - Compensation History Worksheet

Company: _____   Location: _____
Title: _____   Reported to: _____
Start date: _____   End date: _____

Cash compensation

Base salary (starting): _____   Base salary (ending): _____
Target bonus (starting): _____   Actual bonus (starting): _____
Target bonus (ending): _____   Actual bonus (ending): _____
Signing bonus: _____
Other cash compensation: _____

Non-cash compensation

RSUs (average annual value): _____
Options (number): _____
Other (value): _____

Benefits

Paid vacation: _____
Medical: _____
Dental: _____
Life insurance: _____
Long-term disability: _____
401K: _____
Relocation: _____   Value: _____
Temporary housing: _____ Value: _____
Other: _____

Severance

Conditions: _____
Cash: _____
Other: _____

Notes

Module 3 - Focus

1 - The Tao of Focus
2 - Explore
3 - Make a Decision

Module 3 - Focus

In the last Module, we introduced the 3-circle model, inspired by Jim Collins in his best-selling book, Good to Great, which suggests that a good job lies at the intersection of:

- Your career values (or motivations or interests or passions)
- Your career experience (or knowledge, skills, and abilities)
- What the market needs and values

Figure 1 - A good job

You reviewed and reflected on where you've been, considering your **career values**, **career experience**, and **market value**.

In this Module, you'll focus on where you're going (i.e., your next job). To describe your next job, you'll create a Target Job Profile. I've included an example on the next page.

Target Job Profile

Target Position

Industry	software
Industry Segment	analytics software
Function	marketing
Function Segment	product marketing
Vertical Orientation	NA
Size/scale	$25M - $100M
Growth Rate	25% - 100%
Total Staff	1 - 10
Levels Above	1 or 2
Levels Below	1 or 2

Location(s)

Primary	Austin, TX
Secondary	NA

Compensation

Minimum	180K base
Goal	220K base

Market Size Estimates

25 - 35 companies

35 - 50 jobs

Career Values

great product that makes a difference

long-term focus

job autonomy, no micromanging

opportunity for learning and growth

less than 20% travel

work from home 2 days per week

3 weeks vacation

non-execs empowered to make decisions

Example Titles

Chief Marketing Officer (CMO)

Vice President Marketing

Vice President Product Marketing

Example Target Companies

ABC Analytics

DataSoft

XYZ Software and Systems

1 - The Tao of Focus

A few of you may already have sufficient focus to complete a Target Job Profile. If so, you can skip to the end of the Module, fill out your Target Job Profile, and move to the next Module. I've included a Target Job Profile worksheet at the end of this Module.

Most of you, however, will lack sufficient focus and will benefit from working through the process in this Module **before** launching your search.

For many people, getting focused seems counterintuitive and is quite painful. Why eliminate options before you have to? Why not cast a broader net? Who knows what interesting opportunities might pop up? But it seldom works that way.

> *The most important thing I learned from the program was this: the more targeted you are in your search, the more successful you will be. The thought that you might miss an opportunity because you are too narrow in your search can be discomforting. But the reality is that you won't find success, or be happy, if you don't stay true to what you want. Once I got very specific about the companies I was interested in and the role I wanted, the smoother and more successful the job search went. An added benefit of being targeted is that the networking discussions you have go much more smoothly. It becomes the grounds for very specific discussions and enables the person on the other side of the table to help you in a much more specific way.*
>
> James Decker - **Senior Director of Global Strategic Alliances, Innography**

Carl was a senior sales exec who wanted to optimize his chances of finding a job quickly. Carl's story demonstrates how lack of focus impacted his job search.

> During his career, Carl had successfully grown and run large national sales teams. But instead of going to market focused on similarly-sized national roles, Carl decided to cast a broader net and include less senior roles, including 1st-line sales management roles, regional roles, and even sales rep (individual contributor) roles. As a result, he confused the market. If Carl is any good, why would he take a step back and consider subordinate roles? Has he lost his confidence? Did he just get fired? If we offer him a smaller job than he's had, what will he do when a recruiter calls him in two months with a bigger job that pays more money? Carl's lack of focus came across as desperation. After a few

> months, Carl reflected on his values and experience and decided what he really wanted to do (and what he had already done successfully) was build and grow a national sales team in a sales leadership role. He stopped considering subordinate roles and focused his efforts with a consistent message. Almost immediately, opportunities started to present themselves, and Carl was able to land a job within a couple of months.

Remember Russell Diez-Canseco? He wasn't sufficiently focused at first, and he invested several months chasing marshmallows. Then he decided to restart and do it right. Russell focused on two different target jobs, one in education and one in the food industry, but he didn't have a full-time job, and he extended his runway by consulting on the side. Although he initially had two targets, he soon started to gravitate more towards the food industry and then focused most of his energy in that direction.

Get focused **before** you launch your search, and you'll be glad you did.

2 - Explore

To narrow your focus, you'll benefit from exploring jobs in which you're interested, but need to know more about.

Exploring jobs is more than just researching jobs on the Internet. **Exploring includes talking to people who are doing the jobs you want to do and may also involve getting hands-on experience through consulting or projects.** For some, it will entail "day-in-the-life" experiments where you spend a day or two "shadowing" someone who is doing the job in which you're interested.

Exploring jobs is important because most people are myopic with respect to the universe of job opportunities available to them. Furthermore, it's often difficult to get a sense of what it's like working in a different job until you've actually done it. The earlier you are in your career, the more challenging the problem, but even more experienced executives are not immune. One of the most common statements I hear among senior executives goes something like this, "I've had my head down the last four years, running hard in my current job, and I don't know what else is out there." In addition, the degree of specialization, the amount of complexity, and the rate of innovation in the job market has increased, making it harder than ever to "stay on top" of what's going on in other jobs.

James Decker was an executive at a large company, and he wanted to transition to a much smaller company. He had broad functional experience that included marketing, sales, and business development. James spent several months casting a wide net, looking for marketing, sales, and business development roles without getting much traction. To focus his search, James decided to explore three different Target Job Profiles:

- marketing executive for a small company
- sales executive for a small company
- business development executive for a small company

To explore these three different options, James talked to three small company marketing VPs, three small company sales VPs, and three small company business development VPs. During these conversations, James developed a much better sense as to what each of his three target jobs entailed: what was it really like on a day-to-day basis, what skills were essential, what did success look like. He also got feedback on the suitability of his own experience for these jobs - directly from people who were doing the job.

When James started the exploration process, he thought he wanted to be a small company marketing executive. After his conversations, he changed his mind. Not only did he decide that he wanted to be a small company business develop executive, but the people he talked to thought he was a much better fit for a business development role than a marketing role.

Here's a process you can use to start getting focused.

- Narrow your geographic focus.
- Complete up to three Target Job Profiles.
- Research the jobs online.
- Research the jobs by talking to people.
- Conduct experiential research.
- Sanity check the market size.

Narrow Your Geographic Focus

Location is almost always the biggest constraint when conducting a job search. Depending on where you live and what type of job you're looking for, it can be a severe constraint. But it can also be a waste of time to consider jobs that require relocation before deciding whether or not you are able and willing to relocate.

If you have a strong geographic preference (like most people), I suggest initially constraining your exploration to your preferred geography. If the constraint turns out to be too severe, it will become apparent during the exploration process.

It's worth noting that physical location is becoming less relevant in a number of jobs. More people are negotiating commuting arrangements, and more people are working virtually.

Complete Up To Three Target Job Profiles

Use the Target Job Profile worksheet at the end of the Module to define up to three jobs you'd like to explore.

More often than not, your exploration will lead to a preference for one of the target jobs. If a single target job doesn't emerge, you have a couple of choices. You can repeat the process, or you can conduct a job search with more than one target. Unless you can invest 30+ hours per week on your search, I strongly suggest you repeat the process, and try to choose a single target job. In general, it's better to focus on a single target job, change your mind (based on market data and feedback), and then pick another target job later, than it is to try to conduct a search with more than one target job.

If none of your target jobs are of interest, then I suggest you pick 1-3 new target jobs, and run the process again.

> It's better to have eliminated possible target jobs through exploration than to have spent six months (or more) on a job search only to realize the job wasn't of interest, you weren't qualified to do the job, there just weren't many of those jobs available, or the compensation was just not acceptable.

Research the Jobs Online

Thanks to the Internet, it's pretty easy to research jobs online. One method that works well is the top-down approach. Start your research at the industry level, then research interesting companies within the industry, and finally identify people within those companies that are doing jobs of interest to you.

For example, a simple Google search on "fitness industry" filetype:pdf yielded a 34-page analyst report on Fitness and Wellness with a list of leading companies within the industry. You can pick a company from the list (such as Gaiam), go to the company's website, and select SEC Filings for annual reports and other SEC documents. Many of these documents have additional information on the industry and its competitors. A LinkedIn search on Gaiam with Title: marketing yielded 111 people. These are people you might want to speak to about marketing careers in the fitness industry.

Don't neglect social media for research. For example, Gaiam has its own YouTube channel with over 50 videos, and they also have their own Twitter feed @Gaiam and Facebook page.

Research the Jobs by Talking to People

Secondary research (online or in the library) will only get you so far. Probably the best way to learn more about jobs in which you're interested is to talk to people who are currently doing the job. That is exactly what James Decker did to get focused. Here's how to do it:

1. For each Target Job Profile, identify three people who are currently doing the job or who have recently done the job.
2. Contact each person and conduct an informational interview.
3. During the informational interview, focus on:
    a. Developing a sense of what the job actually entails: what is the job like on a day-to-day basis, what experiences are important to do the job well, what are the backgrounds of people in this role, etc.
    b. Understanding the degree to which you are qualified to do the job: does this person believe you are ready to do the job, what are the experience gaps that you will need to overcome, etc.
    c. Determining whether or not this job generally aligns with your values. For example, if one of your values is more balance, and this job requires 90% travel and 90 hours per week, there may be a values mismatch.
    d. Getting a sense of market demand and compensation parameters.

The objective of talking to people who are currently doing jobs that are of potential interest to you is to **better understand exactly what they do**. Below is a list of example questions you might consider using during an informational interview.

1. What is your title?
2. How would you describe your job at a high level?
3. What are the favorite parts of your job?
4. What are the least favorite parts of your job?
5. If you were to allocate the time you spend across three or four primary activities, what are those activities, and roughly what percentage of your time do you spend on each activity?

6. What's on your todo list right now?
7. What's on your calendar for today? Is that a typical day for you? Why or why not?
8. What's on your calendar for this week? Is that a typical week for you? Why or why not?
9. What is the likely career path for you within your current company?
10. What is the likely career path for you if you were to leave your current company?
11. If you are successful in your current role, what will you have accomplished over the next
    a. 6 months,
    b. 12 months,
    c. 24 months,
    d. 36 months?
12. What are the three most important constituencies (other internal groups or organizations, customers, external groups or organizations, shareholders, etc.) to which this job interfaces?
13. Where does your organization sit within the overall company structure?
14. Vis-à-vis this position,
    a. What does your boss do?
    b. What do your peers do?
    c. What do your subordinates do?

Conduct Experiential Research if Necessary

Even if you've talked to 50 people, it's sometimes challenging to envision what a specific job really entails on a day-to-day basis without having ever done the job. If you find yourself interested in a specific job, but it's sufficiently different than anything you've done in your career, experiential research can be enlightening. Consider using experiential research to explore jobs through volunteer efforts, pro bono work, freelance assignments, moonlighting, sabbaticals, and extended vacations. Or try to find someone who is doing the job you want to do and "shadow" them for a day or two.

Sanity Check the Market Size

Many of you will already have an informed sense of the market need for your target job, either because you know the market well or because you've developed a good sense from research and talking to people doing the job. If so, that's great, you can skip this exercise.

But for some of you, this exercise will be useful and save you from wasting time. Perhaps you are moving to a new city, or you've been commuting, or you've had your head down working hard the last several years. Or maybe you just want to sanity check your sense of the market. Whatever the reason, if you need a way to quickly estimate the market need, this exercise should be helpful.

To estimate market demand for a Target Job Profile, first use LinkedIn to see how many people are doing the job you want to do in the city where you want to do it.

For example, let's say I'm targeting CEO jobs for analytics software companies in Austin, TX. I'm interested in small to mid-sized companies, but not a pure startup. I run a LinkedIn search with the following parameters:

- Location = within 50 miles of Austin, TX
- Job Title = CEO
- Industry = Computer Software
- Company Size = 11-500 employees
- Keyword = Analytics

I get 60 hits. Granted, there's some noise in the number, but it gives me a general sense. By contrast, if I run the same search with a location of Tampa, FL, a city roughly the same size as Austin, but with fewer software companies, I only get 12 hits.

Then, if we assume that people change jobs every four years (probably more frequently for small to mid-sized software companies), we can estimate there will be roughly 15 job openings for analytics software companies each year in Austin, TX and 3 job openings each year in Tampa, FL.

Not perfect, but often back-of-the-envelope calculations like this can provide insights that allow us to change our Target Job Profile before we invest too much time looking for a needle in a haystack.

3 - Make a Decision

Before moving on to the next Module, it's important to make a decision and get focused.

> *Keeping your doors open is a trap. It's an excuse to stay uninvolved. I call the people who have the hardest time closing doors Phi Beta Slackers. They hop between esteemed grad schools, fat corporate gigs, and prestigious fellowships, looking as if they have their act together but still feeling like observers, feeling as if they haven't come close to living up to their potential. Phi Beta Slackers are cursed with tremendous ability and infinite choices.*
>
> Po Bronson, bestselling author of <u>What Should I Do With My Life?</u>

Remember, you can always change your mind. That's what I did. I started my job search focused on product marketing roles, but as I explored those jobs, I became less interested. I never would have discovered recruiting sitting in my office.

Use the Target Job Profile worksheet on the next page to make a decision.

Target Job Profile

Target Position

Industry _____

Industry Segment _____

Function _____

Function Segment _____

Vertical Orientation _____

Size/scale _____

Growth Rate _____

Total Staff _____

Levels Above _____

Levels Below _____

Location(s)

Primary _____

Secondary _____

Compensation

Minimum _____

Goal _____

Market Size Estimates

_____

_____

Career Values

_____

_____

_____

_____

_____

Example Titles

_____

_____

_____

Example Target Companies

_____

_____

_____

Notes

Module 4 - Prepare to Launch

1 - Start Building Your Lists
2 - Write a Good Enough Resume
3 - Elevate Your Pitch
4 - Bonus 1: Working With Headhunters
5 - Bonus 2: Using Online Job Sites
6 - Target List Exercise
7 - Target Company List Example
8 - Target Company List Worksheet
9 - Target People List Example
10 - Target People List Worksheet

Module 4 - Prepare to Launch

In the last Module, you completed a Target Job Profile, perhaps exploring various jobs along the way to narrow your focus. In doing so, you embraced the pain of eliminating options. Congratulations! That's a bigger step than you might imagine towards conducting a successful search.

In this Module, you'll prepare to launch your job search. You'll build an initial list of target people and target companies (ten each), and you'll update your resume and LinkedIn profile. I have also included bonus sections on working with recruiters and understanding the real value of online job sites.

But first, a quick refresher.

Job Search Alignment Redux

The power of conducting a targeted job search is that it aligns your search with the way that Hiring Managers fill jobs. To conduct an effective targeted job search, you need to extend your network, and you need to find out about opportunities **before** they turn into posted job openings (before they are broadly socialized). Networking outside of your network and *not* looking for posted jobs may seem counterintuitive at first. For some, it's uncomfortable - perhaps even unnerving. But it's the key to conducting a successful job search.

Let's revisit the story of Kevin from earlier in the book. Remember how he applied these ideas?

> Kevin had been the President of a small division for a mid-sized manufacturing company for just over five years when he decided it was time to make a transition. Kevin heard about a mid-sized manufacturing company that was moving its headquarters from the west coast to his area, so he added that company to his target list of companies. Through online research, he was able to find the name of a potential Hiring Manager within the company. Kevin did not know the Hiring Manager, but he knew someone who knew a potential Influencer (someone who worked for the Hiring Manager). Kevin got a warm introduction to the Influencer and scheduled a phone call with the

> Influencer. This led to a face-to-face meeting with the Influencer and an introduction to the Hiring Manager.
>
> When Kevin met with the Hiring Manager, he found out about several positions the company was trying to fill, but had not yet posted (the positions were being narrowly socialized). Over the course of the ensuing weeks, Kevin spent more time with the Hiring Manager (and other managers at the company) and was ultimately offered a senior operations position.
>
> In the mean time, Kevin had been introduced to the President of another mid-sized manufacturing company (another target company) who was starting to think about replacing the local General Manager (he was still in the formulation phase). As such, there were no other candidates yet for that position. The company moved quickly with Kevin, offered him the job, and Kevin accepted the General Manager position.

The targeted job search process is not particularly complex nor is it difficult to understand. Yet, when executed correctly, it's consistently effective. In many ways, the job search process is similar to the executive recruiting process. In executive recruiting, the most impactful step is to **get the right prospective candidates on the contact list**. If you're soliciting the interest of the wrong candidates, the rest of the process matters little. Similarly, in job search, the most impactful step is to **get the right companies and people on your target lists**. If you bungle this step, the rest of the process won't produce results.

1 - Start Building Your Lists

To launch your search, **you'll need ten people on your target people list and ten companies on your target companies list**. Feel free to add more (you'll likely use them later), but you'll launch your search with ten on each list.

Target companies are companies in which you have an interest regardless of whether or not they have any open positions for which you might be qualified. In fact, it's often better if they do **not** have open positions right now. As we've seen, if they have open positions (that are being broadly socialized), the competition is much greater.

Target people are people who have knowledge of your target industry and are likely to know something about your target companies. They may be Influencers who can make introductions to Hiring Managers and a source of additional companies to add to your list. They are **not** (necessarily) former colleagues or friends whom you know well and are already comfortable meeting for coffee or lunch.

For most knowledge workers and executives, people and companies within your target industry provide the best starting point for building your lists. Why? Because most Hiring Managers consider industry experience to be important when filling key positions (the tip of the tip of the spear).

> If you don't have enough depth to focus on a specific industry, you'll likely want to focus on function or vertical. But doing so will almost always result in a more challenging search. If possible, start with an industry in which you can claim at least some level of experience.

The best way to build your target list of companies and people is to use a combination of secondary (online, published) research and primary (talking to people) research. Most of you will create your list using secondary research, and then refine using primary research.

I've included a Target List Exercise as well as examples and worksheets at the end of this Module.

Here are a few ways to start building your lists.

Broad company databases, such as Hoover's or LinkedIn. I like to start building my target lists with LinkedIn. Use the Advanced Search feature (top center of Home Page) and search for companies by Location, Industry, and Company Size (as an example). Hoover's is great for larger companies, especially if you have a paid subscription (which I did, but I don't anymore). Here is a video I shot in 2011 that demonstrates how I use LinkedIn to build a target list. The fine folks at LinkedIn are always tweaking the user interface, so things may look a bit different today, but the Advanced Search feature is still very similar. As an aside, there are different levels of LinkedIn membership. They include Free, Business, Talent, and Recruiter. If you can afford to do so, I suggest a Business membership at $25/month. The Talent and Recruiter options are more expensive and don't provide any additional features that will help you with your search. Other searchable databases that may be useful include Jigsaw, ZoomInfo, and Spoke.

Niche company databases, such as CrunchBase and Texas TechPulse. There are a number of databases that focus on specific industries or functional areas or types of companies. I'm a tech guy, so I'm most familiar with the tech databases - but they exist in every industry. For example, Texas TechPulse has a searchable database of early-stage tech companies and fundings in Texas. CrunchBase is a national database of tech companies. One of my favorites is the Inc 500 list, a national list of the fastest growing companies in the US. Another is PWC MoneyTree, a searchable database of venture capital activity in the US.

Industry Associations. Virtually every industry has at least one industry association. Most industries have several. I like to use industry associations in a couple of different ways to get target companies. First, many associations have membership directories that can be searched online (some may require a nominal membership fee). Second, industry associations often sponsor big industry events. Companies that co-sponsor events are often good targets as are companies that have speakers at the event.

Analyst reports. Analyst reports typically come in two flavors - industry analyst reports and financial analyst reports. Industry analysts cover the major trends and dynamics within the industry. They may also identify leading companies based on some (non-financial) criteria. Industry analysts for the tech industry include Gartner and Forrester. Financial analysts cover industries or specific public companies within an industry primarily from a financial perspective.

Online Job Sites. While I don't suggest applying to jobs online, some online job sites can be used to develop target lists of companies for your search. For example, you could do an Advanced Search on indeed.com for "virtualization" to see what companies have virtualization-related positions in Austin. If you're interested in virtualization, you may want to add those companies to your list.

Local resources and publications. Virtually every city has a chamber of commerce. Many have publications available for purchase. Some have their own internal databases and may run a search for you. The Austin Chamber of Commerce has run a search for more than one person I've advised. Most cities have a business journal that publishes an annual Book of Lists. These lists often included the largest companies as well as the fastest growing companies across a number of industries.

Libraries. Libraries may have access to premium databases and resources that are too expensive for an individual. In addition, libraries have trained professional researchers! These researchers can help you if you are struggling with your target list. Many larger libraries (such as the University of Texas Libraries) provide online access.

Talk to people. Most people start building their lists using secondary research (published, online), and then add to their lists using primary research (talking to people). But that doesn't mean you can't start your list by talking to people. It just takes more time than starting with secondary research. One person I know built her list entirely by asking people within her target industry for suggestions.

Outsourcing. I don't recommend outsourcing the creation of your target list for a couple of reasons. First, industry and company research is a valuable skill that everyone should develop. Second, there is a lot to be learned through the research process. Outsourcing deprives you of that learning experience. But if you choose to outsource, there are several choices. There are professional researches that work on a project basis. Many of these folks work for recruiters or libraries. They typically charge $40 - $100 per hour. Another possible avenue is trying to find a Library or Information Science student who wants to make some money on the side. There are a ton of them at most major universities.

When in Doubt, Start with One Company

Here's how one person created his initial target lists by starting with a single company.

> *I decided to focus initially on renewable energy as a first industry of interest. In addition, I identified Vestas Wind Systems as one company of great interest within the industry.*
>
> *I used Hoover's to review the company profile on Vestas. Hoover's listed 10 competitors, so I looked at each competitor to see where they were located. For the companies based overseas, I identified the US headquarters. I added those companies to my target list of companies. As a next step, I'll research each of those ten competitors and identify their competitors, etc.*
>
> *I used LinkedIn to run a search on people who work for Vestas in the US. I got 100 hits. I refined the search by adding the criteria of title = project manager (a role in which I was interested). I got 19 hits. Browsing the profiles of the 19 people, I noticed one guy who had recently joined Vestas after completing his MBA at Portland State. I added him to my target people list (people I will contact to request informational interviews). I also scanned the companies for which these people had worked prior to Vestas. It's likely several of those companies will become target companies.*
>
> *Then I used LinkedIn to run a search on people in the Renewables & Environment Industry (one of LinkedIn's industry categories) based in Austin. I got 194 hits. I scanned some of the companies for which they worked and added a couple to my target companies list (RES and Meridian). One of the 194 people was Jose Beceiro, the Director of Clean Energy for the Austin Chamber of Commerce. I added him to my people list. There are probably dozens more than could be good informational sources.*
>
> *Then I used the Companies feature on LinkedIn to search for Vestas. I used the Related Companies function of LinkedIn to identify the most popular career paths for current Vestas employees (some of these companies may become target companies). I also noted the list of companies that the most Vestas employees are connected to (another possible list of target companies). Finally, I used the Key Statistics feature of LinkedIn to note that there are over 100 people employed by Vestas in Portland (one of my target cities).*

But What if I'm Stuck?

Many people find building target lists challenging. If you experience difficulty with developing your target lists, it's probably for one of the following reasons:

- You have not completed the Career Experience Exercise and made key decisions across the nine dimensions of the framework (i.e., you're trying desperately to keep your options open),
- Your target industry is too broadly defined,
- Your target industry is too narrowly defined,
- There are not enough companies in your target industry in your target geographic area (i.e., your target market is too small),
- You haven't invested the time to learn how to use online tools and other resources to build your lists,
- You're spending all of your time chasing marshmallows (i.e., chasing open jobs and trolling the online job sites).

I guarantee that anyone can do this, and it's a valuable 21st century skill worth mastering. Sell-side investment bankers build target lists every time they run a process. They create a list of companies (prospective acquirers) and people (prospective investors). I do it every time I launch an executive search. I create a list of companies (where we're most likely to find qualified candidates) and a list of people (who might be good sources of candidates). I've created a lot of target lists during my recruiting career. Some have been relatively easy, but some have been challenging. It is likely you're going to have to dig a little - maybe a lot - but your target lists really are the foundation of your search.

There is one more point worth mentioning.

> Not only do your target lists provide focus, but they will be the primary discussion documents for many of your networking interactions. If you're not discussing your target list of companies while networking, you'll probably not networking as effectively as you could be (more on this soon).

2 - Write a Good Enough Resume

Virtually everyone already has a resume, but few people have a sense as to whether or not their resume is good or bad. To make matters worse, there are a gazillion experts, each with their own perspectives as to what makes a great resume. A quick search for "resume" on Amazon produces nearly 14,000 books! Here are a few from the top of the list:

- The Resume.Com Guide to Writing UNBEATABLE Resumes
- How to Say It on Your Resume: A Top Recruiting Director's Guide to Writing the PERFECT Resume for Every Job
- Resume MAGIC, 4th Ed: Trade Secrets of a Professional Resume Writer
- KNOCK 'EM DEAD Resumes: Features the Latest Information on: Online Postings, Email Techniques, and Follow-up Strategies
- The Resume Handbook: How to Write OUTSTANDING Resumes and Cover Letters for Every Situation
- The Only Resume and Cover Letter Book You'll Ever Need: 600 RESUMES FOR ALL INDUSTRIES 600 Cover Letters for Every Situation 150 Positions from Entry Level to CEO

Wow! Read a couple of these books, and you'll start to think that the key to landing the perfect job lies in crafting an incredibly awesome resume. My experience, however, leads me to a slightly different conclusion:

- A REALLY GREAT resume will NOT get you a job, but a POORLY DEVELOPED resume may get you disqualified for a job. Your resume is kind of like the clothes you wear to an interview. The best looking suit in the world will not get you the job, but if you show up in jeans and a t-shirt, you might lose the job.
- A great resume will provide transparency into your accomplishments, and it will highlight those accomplishments that best position you for your next career move.
- There's value in redoing your resume to refresh your memory in preparation for interviews. And if you completed the Career Inventory Exercise, you've already done a lot of the leg work.

Rather than bore you with a 300-page resume book, I will offer you a few simple guidelines and a template/example. The guidelines and the resume example should be enough for you to develop a very good resume.

Remove objectives. If you have a Career Objectives section, consider deleting it. It will only serve to potentially eliminate you from consideration for a particular job that is not exactly aligned with your stated objective. Instead of a Career Objectives section, you may want to have a Profile or Summary section that highlights and summarizes accomplishments that are relevant to your next job.

Provide an introductory narrative paragraph. For each position you've held, provide an introductory narrative paragraph. In the introductory narrative paragraph, describe the company for which you worked, its products and/or services, the industry in which it competes, its size, and its location. If you worked for a smaller company or startup, there's a good chance some of your readers will not be familiar with your company. If you worked for a large company like IBM, then describe the relevant business unit or group in which you worked. In addition, describe your "organizational context" within the company. For example, as a VP Marketing, I reported directly to the CEO, managed product marketing, PR, and product management, and had a staff of six. Much of this information should come directly from your Career Experience Worksheet.

Use bullet-pointed accomplishments. Follow the introductory narrative paragraph with a list of quantitative bullet-pointed accomplishments. Here are weak examples: increased revenue 100% (I'm thinking revenue must have been REALLY small since you didn't bother to quantify it); boosted team moral; provided strategic leadership leading to improved performance. Now, compare the weak examples to these much improved examples: increased revenues from $25M to $55M over 20-month period; hired and built team from 3 to 17 over 36 months.

Check your formatting. Be mindful of visual formatting, spelling, and grammar, and use a standard font. Ask a trusted source to check your resume for these items as it is difficult to see errors once you've read your own resume more than a few times. I'm constantly amazed at the number of spelling, grammar, and formatting errors I find in senior executives' resumes. Some formatting errors are caused by the use of non-standard fonts that don't translate well when the resume recipient doesn't have that particular font installed.

Don't worry about size. Size doesn't matter that much. If you follow the format described above, it doesn't matter to me if your resume is two pages or four pages or even longer. But I don't like one-page resumes for mid-level or senior executives: recent college grads and entry-level candidates use one-page resumes.

Be transparent. It's not difficult to tell when someone has omitted information about dates and early career experience in an attempt to conceal their age. My advice is not to do it. Most people see right through it, and it could raise more general concerns about your tendency to conceal information. More important, some companies actually want to hire more experienced employees. If you're transparent, you increase the chances of finding a job that's a good fit.

Don't get fancy. Avoid non-traditional or unusual resume formats. I recommend using a basic chronological resume. Do NOT use a functional resume. Functional resumes disassociate accomplishments from their context, rendering the resume virtually useless. For example, driving an increase in revenue by $10M for a $5M tech startup is different than driving an increase in revenue by $10M for a $500M division of a Fortune 500 company. I also discourage the use of two-column resumes and resumes formatted in landscape mode. Most people will spend very little time on your resume (maybe 15-30 seconds initially). Non-traditional formats make it harder for people to scan your resume quickly.

Omit self assessment. Here are a couple of REAL examples taken from resumes I've received. "My strengths include the ability to quickly seek out cause-effect relationships to identify the root cause of problems." "Visionary, resourceful, and highly accomplished leader." These comments provide no real value. In lieu of self assessment, show results with quantifiable accomplishments as mentioned above.

Do it, proof it, move on. When it's done, it's done. Make sure you spell check, grammar check, and format check, and show it to a few friends to get their feedback. But, resist the temptation to keep making small tweaks after it's done.

You may want to have a professional resume writer help you with your resume. That's fine, as long as you make a first attempt at your resume yourself. Good resume writers are particularly adept at listening to your career history, pulling out accomplishments that are relevant, and quantifying those accomplishments in a compelling way. If you want a real pro to help you (for a fee of course), talk to Liz Handlin at <u>Ultimate Resumes</u>. Liz is the best I've worked with, and her idea of a good resume coincides closely with mine. You can contact Liz at liz.handlin@ultimateresumes.com.

John Doe

1234 Technology Lane
Austin, Texas 78701

512 555-1234
john@doe.com

PROFILE

- 25 years of experience in high-tech marketing roles with a technical undergrad.
- Proven experience leading marketing for early-stage tech companies with strong functional experience in product marketing, strategic marketing, and product management.

EXPERIENCE

Newco Software Company, City, State — April 2006 - present
Vice President Marketing

Newco Software is a private venture-backed middleware company. Founded in 1998, Newco has raised $15M in venture funding from HT Ventures and ABC Capital. The company's products focus on a middleware integration platform for financial services companies. As Vice President of Marketing, I report directly to the CEO and have responsibility for strategic marketing, product marketing, product management, and marketing communications.

- Manage marketing staff of 5 and marketing budget of $1.5M.
- First member of marketing group – hired entire marketing team. No turnover in marketing group.
- Developed PRD for 1st and 2nd generation products.
- Developed relationships with analysts from Gartner and Forrester.
- Developed messaging and competitive positioning strategy.
- Along with CEO, participated in all roadshow presentations for A round and B round funding.

ACME Widget, City, State — February 2002 - April 2006
Vice President Marketing and Business Development

ACME Widget is a lorem ipsum dolor sit amet, usu te ornatus referrentur, saepe tritani erroribus per ut. Ne sed tota consul, te eum oblique alienum. Homero aliquid adipiscing usu no. Labore eirmod ocurreret has id, vocent pericula disputationi et sea. No case idque repudiandae mei, te aeque utroque sensibus mel. Omnis omnesque scribentur eam ne, nec in ignota iriure invenire, nemore legimus qui te.

- Managed blah blah blah blah blah blah blah blah blah blah blah blah blah.
- Drove blah blah blah blah blah blah blah blah blah blah blah blah blah
- Developed blah blah blah blah blah blah blah blah blah blah blah blah blah
- Created blah blah blah blah blah blah blah blah blah blah blah blah blah
- Built blah blah blah blah blah blah blah blah blah blah blah blah blah

Mid Market High Tech Company, City, State — October 1997 - January 2002
Director Marketing

Mid Market is a lorem ipsum dolor sit amet, usu te ornatus referrentur, saepe tritani erroribus per ut. Ne sed tota consul, te eum oblique alienum. Homero aliquid adipiscing usu no. Labore eirmod ocurreret has id, vocent pericula disputationi et sea. No case idque repudiandae mei, te aeque utroque sensibus mel. Omnis omnesque scribentur eam ne, nec in ignota iriure invenire, nemore legimus qui te.

- Managed blah blah blah blah blah blah blah blah blah blah blah blah blah.
- Drove blah blah blah blah blah blah blah blah blah blah blah blah blah
- Developed blah blah blah blah blah blah blah blah blah blah blah blah blah
- Created blah blah blah blah blah blah blah blah blah blah blah blah blah
- Built blah blah blah blah blah blah blah blah blah blah blah blah blah

Another Fortune 500 Company, City, State　　　　　　　　　　August 1992 - October 1997
Marketing Manager

Another F500 Company is a lorem ipsum dolor sit amet, usu te ornatus referrentur, saepe tritani erroribus per ut. Ne sed tota consul, te eum oblique alienum. Homero aliquid adipiscing usu no. Labore eirmod ocurreret has id, vocent pericula disputationi et sea. No case idque repudiandae mei, te aeque utroque sensibus mel. Omnis omnesque scribentur eam ne, nec in ignota iriure invenire, nemore legimus qui te.

- Managed blah blah blah blah blah blah blah blah blah blah blah blah blah.
- Drove blah blah blah blah blah blah blah blah blah blah blah blah blah
- Developed blah blah blah blah blah blah blah blah blah blah blah blah blah
- Created blah blah blah blah blah blah blah blah blah blah blah blah blah
- Built blah blah blah blah blah blah blah blah blah blah blah blah blah

Big Fortune 500 Company, City, State　　　　　　　　　　　　July 1986 - July 1990
Marketing and Sales Associate

Big Fortune 500 Company is a lorem ipsum dolor sit amet, usu te ornatus referrentur, saepe tritani erroribus per ut. Ne sed tota consul, te eum oblique alienum. Homero aliquid adipiscing usu no. Labore eirmod ocurreret has id, vocent pericula disputationi et sea. No case idque repudiandae mei, te aeque utroque sensibus mel. Omnis omnesque scribentur eam ne, nec in ignota iriure invenire, nemore legimus qui te.

- Managed blah blah blah blah blah blah blah blah blah blah blah blah blah.
- Drove blah blah blah blah blah blah blah blah blah blah blah blah blah
- Developed blah blah blah blah blah blah blah blah blah blah blah blah blah
- Created blah blah blah blah blah blah blah blah blah blah blah blah blah
- Built blah blah blah blah blah blah blah blah blah blah blah blah blah

EDUCATION

The Cache Graduate School of Business, City, State
MBA Finance　　　　　　　　　　　　　　　　　　　　　　　　　　　　　1992

TopNotch College, City, State
BS Electrical Engineering　　　　　　　　　　　　　　　　　　　　　　　1986

PROFESSIONAL ACTIVITIES

Director - High Tech Council　　　　　　　　　　　　　　　　　　　　2001 - 2008

Member - ABC Local Chapter　　　　　　　　　　　　　　　　　　　2006 - present
Advisory Board Member - ACME Widget　　　　　　　　　　　　　2008 - present

3 - Elevate Your Pitch

Everyone can benefit from an elevator pitch that lasts between 30 and 60 seconds. Your elevator pitch is *not* something you typically use in an interview. Rather, you use it when networking to allow your network to better help you. I recommend that you have both a verbal and written version of your elevator pitch, and they should be similar.

Your elevator pitch is also a great way to solicit the feedback of other people regarding the clarity and conciseness of your job focus. If you spend 30-60 seconds describing what type of job you're looking for, but other people just don't get it, chances are you have some work to do on your pitch (or you need more focus).

Here's a simple formula that's effective for most people who are changing jobs, but not making a major career shift (i.e., looking for a completely different type of job in a different industry in a different functional role).

- Describe your current (or most recent) position. Include the industry, functional role, and size of company. Include vertical orientation if relevant.
- Add one line that provides an example or color around your responsibilities in that position.
- Describe the job you're looking for with the same format you used to describe your current (or most recent) position above (industry, functional role, size of company, and vertical orientation if relevant). Include geographic preferences or constraints.

Here's an example:

> *Hi, I'm John Doe. Most recently I ran sales for ACME Systems, a $50M company that sells software to large oil and gas companies. I was responsible for hunting and closing many of the company's big multi-million dollar deals. I'm looking for a job running sales for a mid-size software company in Texas.*

Your online persona

Have you searched for yourself on Google? Think of your online persona as what pops up when you conduct a search on yourself. You will probably see some or all of the following:

- LinkedIn profile
- Twitter profile
- Facebook page
- Google+
- Blog entries
- Press releases
- Website bio
- Photos and images
- Videos
- All sorts of bizarre stuff about other people with the same name

Some of these you can change (LinkedIn profile), but others you cannot. You should assume that companies in which you are interested will, at a minimum, invest the time to do a Google search on you and read through some of the information. Many Hiring Managers will do a LinkedIn search to view (and perhaps call) mutual connections. Many of my recruiting clients are using this information to conduct more extensive research and background checks.

For non-changeable elements of your online persona, the key is just to be aware of what's out there so you don't get blindsided. If there's information on Twitter or Facebook that you'd prefer not to share, make sure your profiles are private.

The world has changed. Don't get caught off guard!

In general, I recommend updating what you can and being aware of the rest.

- Make sure your LinkedIn profile is consistent with your resume. As obvious as it sounds, I have found executives with numerous inconsistencies, including employment dates and job omissions.

- Including as much detail in your LinkedIn profile as what is on your resume is generally a good idea. Many people will view your LinkedIn profile before they see your resume.
- Check for multiple versions of your LinkedIn profile, and delete old or outdated versions.
- If appropriate, take advantage of LinkedIn's features to include presentations and videos.
- Don't get too caught up in getting people to write recommendations on your LinkedIn profile. If you do have recommendations, they should be specific, as quantifiable as possible, and provide examples. The more relevant they are to the type of job you're looking for, the better. Recommendations from former superiors are especially relevant. Focus on quality, not quantity.

4 - Bonus 1: Working With Headhunters

head·hunt·er
/ˈhedˌhən(t)ər/
noun: headhunter; plural noun: headhunters
1. a person who identifies and approaches suitable candidates employed elsewhere to fill business positions.
2. a member of a society that collects the heads of dead enemies as trophies.

Headhunters come in a variety of shapes and forms. It's useful to know which type of headhunter you're dealing with. They can be helpful to you, a complete waste of time, or perhaps even dangerous.

How Recruiters Work

There are two main types of recruiters - retained and contingency. Over the last several years, a third type has emerged - contained recruiters - which are a hybrid of retained and contingent. They work in different ways, have different incentives, and have different business models.

Retained Recruiters

Retained recruiters typically focus on executive-level positions, and they are paid a retainer (monthly fee) by their client (the company doing the hiring) to provide advice and fill one specific role. The search firm's relationship with their client is exclusive; they are the only firm working on the search. Retained recruiters work for retained executive search firms. The largest of these firms include Korn/Ferry, Heidrick & Struggles, Spencer Stuart, and Egon Zehnder. There are also a myriad of smaller, boutique executive search firms that typically specialize within an industry or functional area.

The executive search industry is very fragmented with over 10,000 firms. While the largest firms have hundreds of millions of dollars in annual revenue, firms at the bottom of the top 20 list may have $25M or less, so it's a very long-tail, fragmented industry. Put another way, the largest firms handle a very small percentage of all searches. Retained recruiters focus on filling a relatively small number of positions, and they complete a very high percentage of searches on which they work. They won't "shop you around" in hopes of getting a fee, and they won't help you find a job. Successful retained recruiters are maniacally focused on two things: doing business development to generate new searches and more revenue, and filling a very small number of positions with the best possible candidates. ***Retained recruiters have no direct monetary interest in helping you find a job.***

Contingency Recruiters
Contingency recruiters focus on mid-level down to entry-level positions. Whereas retained recruiters are paid a retainer on a monthly basis throughout the course of a search assignment, contingency recruiters are paid if and only if the search is completed. In other words, their fee is contingent upon one of their candidates accepting the job. Contingency recruiters may or may not have an exclusive relationship with their client, so there may be several contingency recruiters trying to fill the same position.

Contingency firms are also competing directly against their clients, who may be sourcing their own candidates in parallel. This means that if you contact a Hiring Manager directly regarding a position that a contingency recruiter is also trying to fill, your chances might be better because the Hiring Manager won't pay a fee if you're hired. Contingency firms may fill only a small percentage of searches on which they work, but that's fine because they are usually working on lots of searches at any given time. Unlike retained firms, contingency firms may offer to "shop you around" to a few of their clients that they believe might be interested. Unscrupulous firms have been known to shop around resumes without candidates' permission.

Contained Recruiters
Contained recruiters typically charge a small retainer up front, but receive the bulk of their fee only if one of their candidates is hired. As such, their incentives and behaviors are more similar to contingency recruiters than retained recruiters.

If you are contacted by a recruiter, find out what type they are and who they work for. Legitimate recruiters will be happy to answer questions if you ask them.

How to Best Leverage Recruiters

Most sources indicate that recruiters fill about 5% of all jobs, but I suspect the percentage is much smaller, especially for executive and management positions. I think the percentage is probably more like 2%. Regardless, your chances of finding a job through a recruiter are slim.

Even if you are solicited directly by a recruiter for a specific job, the odds are stacked against you. A good recruiter may solicit the interest of 100-200 candidates for a single job, and most of the candidates will be well-qualified (at least on paper).

> *The best jobs are the ones that certainly haven't gone out to an executive recruiter. The reason these are the 'best' jobs for you is that once it goes to an executive recruiter there will be a stack of 100 prospective recruits, 20 amazingly qualified resumes that will have phone or in-person interviews with the recruiter of which the company will meet 5-6. So unless your last job is a mirror image of your next, then good luck with those odds.*
>
> Mark Suster - General Partner, GRP Partners

So, if your chances of finding a job through a recruiter are slim, what's the best way to leverage them? **The answer is to treat them like anyone else on your target people list.**

Recruiters may be able to provide information on your target companies and perhaps even make introductions. **In other words, recruiters may play the role of Influencers when networking your way into companies.** Instead of sending your resume to a recruiter and asking her to "let you know if she hears of anything," try to engage the recruiter in a conversation focused on your target industry segments and specific target companies. We'll cover this in more detail next week.

When engaging a recruiter in this way, I suggest the following approach:

- Send your resume before the call
- Give your elevator pitch instead of "walking through the resume"
- Describe the segments or types of companies you're targeting (i.e., I'm looking at SaaS companies in the 10M – 25M range based in Texas)
- Mention a few of the companies on your target list
- Ask the recruiter about those companies

- Ask the recruiter if there are similar companies you might consider adding to your list
- Ask the recruiter how you can be helpful and then follow through
- Ask the recruiter what is the best way to keep in touch
- Offer to help with current searches (but don't suggest candidates unless they are a strong fit)

Recruiter Rules of Thumb

Here are a few general rules of thumb to keep in mind when working with recruiters.

Build it before you need it. Build your network of recruiters before you need it. When a recruiter contacts you, always respond. If you are not looking for a job, let the recruiter know, and ask the recruiter how you can be helpful. If you are looking for a job, but are not interested in the job the recruiter is currently trying to fill, let the recruiter know, and ask the recruiter how you can be helpful. Check out the recruiter online if you don't already know the recruiter. The search firm should have a website with direct contact information, and the recruiter should have a LinkedIn profile. Google the recruiter's name to see what pops up. Make sure you are connected through LinkedIn to the recruiters you already know.

Cast a broad net. When working with recruiters at the big firms, or even at smaller firms with multiple Partners, do *not* assume that recruiters within the firm will share your credentials with other recruiters within the firm. Maybe they will, but usually they will not. Because of the way Partners are compensated at most executive search firms, they actually compete with other Partners in the same firm. **Not only do they compete with other Partners for the same clients, but they also compete for the same candidates.** In many search firms, if a Partner is soliciting the interest of a candidate for a search, the Partner "locks" the candidate for his/her own use in the firm's database. That candidate can only be approached by other recruiters within the firm after she is "unlocked." In my experience, there are a few firms that truly collaborate internally, but most do not. My advice is to talk to all of the recruiters within a firm that make sense for you given your areas of interest.

Show the Associates some love. Don't overlook the Associates. Partners make rain and manage client relationships, but the Associates do most of work. Even if you're looking for a CEO position, don't assume the Partner is doing the heavy lifting. Usually, they are not. In the larger search firms, most Partners focus exclusively on business development. An experienced Partner at a big firm or larger boutique firm may have 1 or 2 Junior Partners (or Principals), 2 to 4 Associates, and 2 to 4 Researchers as part of her team. The Associates are the ones who do the heavy lifting and solicit most of the candidates. Get to know the good ones, and try to be helpful to them.

Don't waste the recruiter's time. Be transparent from day one about your level of interest in a specific role. If it's not a fit for you, let the recruiter know, and offer to refer other candidates if you're in a position to do so. The recruiter will appreciate your candor. It's also useful to let the recruiter know why the position is not of interest to you. Perhaps you're under a misconception regarding the position, or perhaps you don't have all of the information necessary to determine fit. If so, the recruiter may be able to clarify the role, and upon clarification, you may decide the position could be a fit for you after all.

5 - Bonus 2: Using Online Job Sites

Like recruiters, online job sites can be helpful in your search if you know how they work and understand how to best leverage them.

How Online Job Sites Work

Online job sites collect applications and/or resumes and distribute them to the organization that posted the job. That's not the problem. The problem is what happens when the applications/resumes are received by the hiring organization.

> A few years ago, I got a call from a friend of a friend who was an intern in the HR department of a well-known company. The intern called me for some advice. His boss was the departmental head of HR, and she had asked him to screen the 250 or so resumes that had been submitted online for a management position. His boss needed the top ten candidates by the next day. The intern wanted to know what to do. What do you think are the chances this intern picked the ten best qualified people for the job? Or, even one or two of the ten best qualified people for the job? Submitting your resume for a job through an online job site is an imperfect process, and there is little or no feedback provided. Often, HR subordinates filter the initial set of resumes, not the Hiring Manager. Knowing how online job sites work, or more specifically, knowing how resumes from online job sites are typically screened, you can see why people who focus their job search on online job sites tend to experience high levels of frustration.

How to Best Leverage Online Job Sites

Here's my two cents on online job sites. **Never apply for a job online, even if you think you're a fit**. Instead, do some research, determine who the Hiring Manager is, and approach the Hiring Manager directly (more on this soon). Applying for a job online is not only inefficient and ineffective, but it can also be frustrating: you know you're qualified, but you never hear back. **The only value of online job sites is that they often contain data that can support your job search.** Specifically, online job sites allow you to do research in the following ways:

- Get a sense as to which companies hire people like you;

- Get a sense as to what companies are hiring or growing and therefore might be worthy of research and potentially adding to your target list;
- Search for jobs at companies on your target list to gain a sense of what they're up to. For example, if your search for ACME Widget reveals they are looking to hire five social media experts, you can probably assume one of ACME's key initiatives has something to do with social media;
- Get a sense of what segments are hot and perhaps worth investigating further, and which segments are not so hot. For example, a search on Indeed.com for "social media" produced 275 jobs. A search on "virtualization" produced 598 jobs. A search on fabless semiconductors produced 8 jobs;
- Search the total number of jobs in different geographic areas to get a relative sense of job market size;
- Use the "Trends" feature on Indeed.com to identify what careers or industry segments are the most popular;
- Use the "Job Postings per Capita" feature on Indeed.com if you're considering relocation. This feature allows you to see that there is one job posting per one unemployed person in Washington DC, but only one job opening per six unemployed people in Miami, FL.

Spend time on online job sites for research purposes only. Focus on the data and information-intensive parts of the sites. Resist the temptation to apply for jobs online unless you've already spoken to the Hiring Manager and the job requires applying online.

6 - Target List Exercise

I consider your target list of companies and your target list of people to be the two most impactful documents you'll use during your search. They form the foundation of the job search process. It's important to make sure you create your initial lists before moving on to the next Module.

1) Create a target list of 10 companies. If you have more than 10, prioritize the top 10. **Target companies** are companies in which you have an interest regardless of whether or not they have any open positions for which you might be qualified. In fact, it's often better if they do NOT have open positions right now. As we've seen, if they have open positions (that are being broadly socialized), the competition is much greater.

2) Note the companies on your list that are sufficiently large that they may have multiple organizations (or business units) that might have jobs available for people like you.

3) Write a short paragraph or a couple of sentences describing the companies on your list. For example - *my initial list is comprised of software companies, headquartered in Texas, with revenue between 25M - 100M, that sell to big companies.*

4) Create a target list of 10 people. If you have more than 10, prioritize the top 10. **Target people** are people who have knowledge of your target industry and are likely to know something about your target companies. They may be Influencers who can make introductions to Hiring Managers and a source of additional companies to add to your list. They are NOT (necessarily) former colleagues or friends who you know well and are already comfortable meeting for coffee or lunch. Remember, it's important to extend your network.

5) Write a short paragraph or a couple of sentences describing the people on your list.

7 - Target Company List Example

	Company	Location	Website	Industry/sector	Size
1	ACME Fitness	LA	www.acmefit.com	fitness training	10M - 50M
2	SocialFitness.com	LA	www.socialfitness.com	fitness products	0M - 10M
3	ACME Wellness	LA	www.acmewell.com	fitness training	0M - 10M
4	ABC Training	LA	www.abdtraining.com	fitness training	0M - 10M
5	XYZ Sports Medicine	LA	www.xyzsports.com	fitness products	0M - 10M
6	ACME Widget	Austin	www.acmewidget.com	fitness products	10M - 50M
7	Health Corp	LA	www.healthcorp.com	fitness products	50M - 250M
8	Fitness Guru	LA	www.firnessguru.com	fitness training	0M - 10M
9	WellFit	LA	www.wellfit.com	fitness training	0M - 10M
10	FitKids	LA	www.fitkids.com	fitness training	10M - 50M
11					
12					
13					
14					
15					
16					
17					
18					
19					
20					
21					
22					
23					
24					
25					
26					
27					
28					
29					
30					

8 - Target Company List Worksheet

	Company	Location	Website	Industry/sector	Size
1					
2					
3					
4					
5					
6					
7					
8					
9					
10					
11					
12					
13					
14					
15					
16					
17					
18					
19					
20					
21					
22					
23					
24					
25					
26					
27					
28					
29					
30					

9 - Target People List Example

	Name	Title	Company	Industry/sector	Connection
1	John Doe	VP Sales	FitSpring	fitness training	2nd
2	Sally Doe	VP Sales	Ultra Fit	fitness products	2nd
3	Ralph Doe	Dir Marketing	T-Devices	fitness training	2nd
4	Jane Doe	Advisor	Ultra Fit	fitness training	1st
5	Jimmy Doe	Board Member	MyFitShoes	fitness products	2nd
6	Jenny Doe	CEO	iWearables	fitness products	2nd
7	Bob Doe	VP Sales	Rouge Fitness	fitness products	2nd
8	Steve Doe	VP Services	Mega Cross	fitness training	1st
9	Rick Doe	Consultant	NuFit	fitness training	2nd
10	Peggy Doe	Attorney	Doe & Associates	legal	1st
11					
12					
13					
14					
15					
16					
17					
18					
19					
20					
21					
22					
23					
24					
25					
26					
27					
28					
29					
30					

10 - Target People List Worksheet

	Name	Title	Company	Industry/sector	Connection
1					
2					
3					
4					
5					
6					
7					
8					
9					
10					
11					
12					
13					
14					
15					
16					
17					
18					
19					
20					
21					
22					
23					
24					
25					
26					
27					
28					
29					
30					

Notes

Module 5 - Execute

1 - Run a Process
2 - Use 30-Day Sprints
3 - Track Your Progress
4 - Target Company Research Checklist
5 - Weekly Scorecard
6 - Weekly Scorecard Example

Module 5 - Execute

You've made important decisions about what type of job you'll pursue, built and prioritized your initial list of target companies and people, updated your resume and LinkedIn profile, and polished your elevator pitch.

Now it's time to launch and execute your search.

To execute a successful job search, you need to **run a process**. Investment bankers run a process when they are trying to sell a company because a process generates more buyers, maximizes valuation, and helps find buyers with aligned interests. Executive recruiters run a process when they are trying to fill a key executive position because a process generates more candidates, uncovers the most qualified candidates, and provides the perspective needed to select the best candidate available. People who want more from their careers run a process when they are navigating transitions because a process prepares them well for a successful search, results in more and better opportunities, and provides mechanisms to course correct if needed. The process you'll learn is rigorous, targeted, and proactive. By contrast, most people navigate transitions in a more arbitrary, scattered, and reactive manner. You'll use 30-day sprints to focus your efforts and Weekly Scorecards to track your activity as well as your progress.

1 - Run a Process

Remember, the power of conducting a targeted job search is that it aligns your search with the way that Hiring Managers fill jobs. To conduct an effective targeted job search, you need to extend your network, and you need to find out about opportunities before they turn into posted job openings (before they are broadly socialized).

You'll do this by networking your way towards Hiring Managers in your target companies, leveraging people in your existing network (in orange below), but also creating new connections and extending your network (in gray below).

I call this process ***targeted networking***.

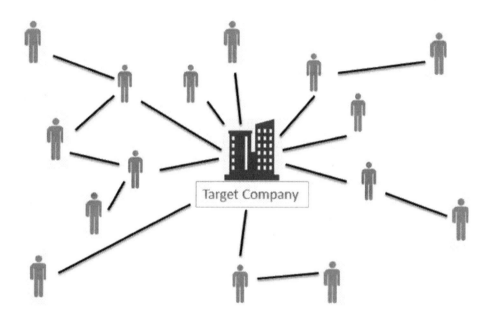

Targeted networking helps you get in front of Hiring Managers in your target companies. The process is comprised of four main steps. Repeat the process for every company on your target list until you find a great job.

1. Find out as much as you can about the company.
2. Develop a Point of View (PoV) as to where and how you fit within the company.
3. Identify specific Hiring Managers and Influencers.
4. Network your way into the company and connect with Hiring Managers.

Even if the company you're targeting is actively trying to fill a specific role and has posted the job or is using a recruiter, your best chance of rising above the noise and getting the job is to connect directly with the Hiring Manager. **Hiring Managers make hiring decisions**, not recruiters or HR executives or entry-level associates who filter resumes from job boards. To be clear, it doesn't mean you should circumvent a recruiter if your interest in a job is solicited, but it does mean that you should always be trying to network your way toward Hiring Managers of interest.

Let's look at each of the four steps of the execution process in more detail. I've included a Target Company Research Checklist at the end of this Module.

Step 1 - Find Out as Much as You Can About the Company

Find out as much as you can about your target companies using online research first, followed by a couple of phone calls with insiders to get the real story on what's going on in the company. Company research helps prepare you for subsequent conversations, meeting, and interviews.

Here are some suggestions for researching a company online:

- **Check out the company's website.** Familiarize yourself with the company's products and/or services. What do they sell and to whom? Are there specific vertical markets? Read through the bios of the key executives and board members. Check out recent press releases. Sometimes there will be analyst reports you can download for free that show how the company is positioned vis-a-vis competitors. If there is an events page, see what recent events the company has attended. Go to the event website and see what other companies attended the event to get a sense of competitors and partners.

- **Search for relevant videos.** Check out YouTube and Vimeo, and use a video search engine to see what's out there. Google indexes different video sites than Bing, so check out both. It's likely you'll learn more from non-professional videos than from highly choreographed, professional type videos that you might find on the company's website. I like to search for the company name as well as the names of a few key executives. Here's a cool video of Brett Hurt, founder and former CEO of Bazaarvoice, that was shot at a bar/restaurant in 2008. Very informal and unscripted, but very useful.

- **Try to get a sense of the size of the company.** If the company is public, it's easy. If the company is private, try Hoover's or LinkedIn for an estimate of revenues and number of employees.

- **Try to find relevant industry or financial analyst reports.** Public companies often list analysts on the investor page of the company website. You can also check out recent annual reports. Private companies may require more digging.

- **Play around on Google (or your favorite search engine) and see what pops up.** I like to search for PDF and PPT documents. Sometimes you'll get lucky and find recent presentations or even investor pitches. For example, do a Google search on Bazaarvoice, and you'll see the company website, Facebook page, Glassdoor reviews, CrunchBase page, Twitter page, and LinkedIn page. Pretty boring. But try a Google search with filetype PDF or PPT, and you'll find much more interesting content.

- **Use real-time social media to track the company.** Set a Google alert, a LinkedIn alert, "friend" the company on Facebook, and follow the company and key executives on Twitter and LinkedIn.

- **Try to get the organizational "lay-of-the-land".** Try to get a sense of how the company is structured organizationally. Is the company organized around functions or business units or geographies, or is it a hybrid? Sometimes high-level org charts are available online. Identify all organizations that might be a fit for you.

- **Visit Glassdoor.** Check out Glassdoor.com to get an insider's view on your target companies.

You can find out a lot about a company these days through online research, but it's still useful to talk to people directly to get a sense of what's *really* going on within your target companies.

People who might be good sources of information include:

- Former employees (often the best source if you can find them)
- People you know within the same industry as your target company
- Service providers or partners that may know the company
- Peer-level or subordinate-level employees currently at the company (but only if you know them well)

Gathering information on one of your target companies at this stage is kind of like doing a "back channel" candidate reference check. You're talking to people with a working knowledge of the company and trying to better understand the following:

- What's working well at the company
- What's not working so well
- How did the company do this past year vs. its projections
- How did the company do this past year vs. its competitors
- Biggest opportunities for the company
- Biggest challenges facing the company
- Industry trends
- New products or services
- New key executive hires
- Upcoming events, conferences, and presentations
- Names of other people that have worked there or currently work there
- Where you might fit within the company on an organizational basis
- How you might fit within the company on a cultural basis
- What skills and/or experiences the company values most
- What Hiring Managers you might want to connect with
- What Influencers you might want to talk to

As you collect more data points and intelligence about the company, use subsequent conversations to confirm or dispel your information.

Step 2 - Develop a Point of View (PoV) as to Where and How You Fit

One of the primary reasons you're doing all this research is to better understand how you might be able to help your target companies as an employee. You want to be able to walk into a meeting with a Hiring Manager and have an informed hypothesis as to the needs of the company and how and where you fit in. When a Hiring Manager meets a candidate who has taken the time to research the company and developed a thoughtful point of view, that candidate distinguishes himself or herself from the myriad of other candidates. *I can tell you that every company, no matter how successful or popular, faces challenges recruiting the right people.*

Let's say you're a sales exec and ACME is one of your targets. Your online research makes it clear that ACME is growing, has just raised another round of funding, and is poised to grow even faster during the next year. You noticed that the last three press releases on the ACME website are about new customers in the oil & gas vertical. Through a conversation with a friend who knows something about ACME, you confirm your suspicion that ACME is beginning to develop a sales strategy focused on new vertical markets, and one of the key verticals is oil & gas. While your vertical sales experience is broader than just oil & gas, compared to the average sales exec, you have a significant amount of oil & gas experience. It seems that ACME could use someone like you with deep oil & gas experience as it continues its growth in that vertical. In your conversations with the ACME Hiring Manager, you make sure to highlight your experience in oil & gas.

If there happens to be a specific job opening for which you believe you are a good fit, that's great. This process still works. Try to understand the specific job responsibilities and outcomes before you start selling yourself. Also, don't assume that just because a job has been "posted" that the Hiring Manager has adequately defined the job and knows what he's looking for. Similarly, don't assume that there aren't other related jobs that have not been formally posted, but for which you might be an even better fit. Resist the temptation to slip back into "sell mode" even for posted positions.

> Ken Kuznia is a former executive recruiter and creator of [DigYourWork](). Ken tells a powerful story about how his best executive recruiting candidates were getting rejected by clients even though they were well-qualified for the jobs for which they were

> interviewing. Ken discovered that when his candidates started asking themselves, "What's in it for the company?" or "How can I help this company?" instead of, "What's in it for me?", his placement rates immediately went up by 300%! Ken refers to this change in perspective as the Paradigm Shift.
>
> The Paradigm Shift embodies the notion that finding a great job is *less* about promoting yourself more effectively or more aggressively and *more* about first understanding a company's opportunities and challenges, and then articulating how and where you fit, if at all.

The Paradigm Shift mindset should not only guide you through developing your PoV about your target companies, but it should also guide you through all of your conversations and meetings as you enter the execution phase of the process. Don't over promote yourself. Don't monopolize conversations with stories of your accomplishments. Don't email unsolicited resumes. Don't assume you know what the job entails even if you have a job spec. **Stop talking, and start listening.** Put on your detective's hat, and use every conversation and interaction as an opportunity to ask questions and learn more about your target companies. You're not just looking for a job; you're looking for a problem to solve that aligns with your skills and experience and interests.

Ken was kind enough to share the Paradigm Shift story with us at a special lunch presentation. You can watch the video here.

Step 3 - Identify Specific Hiring Managers and Influencers

Ultimately, you'll need to connect with Hiring Managers to secure a job. The first step is identifying who those Hiring Managers might be. In smaller companies, you may be able to readily identify relevant Hiring Managers directly through research, while in larger companies you may have to network a bit to find them.

If you haven't already done so, this would be a great time to build your LinkedIn network by adding people you know who are *not* already part of your LinkedIn network. I'm not suggesting you connect to people that you don't know, but if you're like me, you probably know a lot of people who you're not connected to on LinkedIn. Select Add Connections in the upper right corner of the LinkedIn home page. If you use Outlook,

Apple Mail, or another email application, you may be able to import your contacts automatically.

While your goal is to connect directly with Hiring Managers, in most cases your strategy will be to network your way towards the Hiring Manager by connecting first with key Influencers. Even if you already know the Hiring Manager well, I believe there are often advantages to not contacting him/her immediately, namely the information and intelligence you'll gain from speaking to Influencers first.

> Remember that Influencers are those people close to a Hiring Manager who are tapped to see if they know of any good candidates before a position is broadly socialized.

For most target companies on your list, key Influencers will include:

- Current employees, especially peers to HMs, superiors to HMs, and subordinates to HMs
- Former employees, especially peers to HMs, superiors to HMs, and subordinates to HMs
- Trusted external advisors, consultants, bankers, attorneys. recruiters, etc.
- Board members, board advisors, board observers
- Ecosystem partners (suppliers, channels, vendors, etc.)

The best way to identify an initial list of Influencers is by using LinkedIn. Using the Advanced Search feature, specify the name of your target company in the Company field. Sort the results by Relationship to see who you're connected to. By default, LinkedIn will display the profiles of all Current as well as Past employees. You may want to focus initially on Past employees, as they are often in a position to speak more openly.

For each Hiring Manager in each target company, try to identify 3 - 5 key Influencers who can help you network your way towards the Hiring Manager.

Step 4 - Network Your Way Into the Company and Connect With Hiring Managers

The primary goal of networking your way into one of your target companies is to engage in discussions with people who are in a position to offer you a job (Hiring Managers). You may be interviewing for a specific position, or it may be a more informal meeting, or you may think it's an informal meeting but the Hiring Manager has a specific role in mind. Regardless, *your goal is to get a face-to-face meeting with a Hiring Manager and have a substantive conversation about the company, where you might fit, and how you might be able to help*. When you reach the point of meeting with a Hiring Manager, and there is a specific job that you are discussing, you are ready to move to the Assessment phase of the process (next Module).

A secondary goal of targeted networking, but in some ways an equally important goal, is to learn as much about the company as you can *before* you meet with Hiring Managers. You may only get one shot with a Hiring Manager, and you want to be as prepared and informed as possible.

Networking Strategy - Who to Talk to and Why

There are three types of people with whom you'll be networking: specific target company Influencers who you identified in step 3, people on your Target People List, and everyone else. Let's consider each separately.

- **Specific target company Influencers.** Ideally, you'll work your way "up the food chain" within your target companies before connecting directly with a Hiring Manager. You might start with non-employees, then peer level employees, then Hiring Managers. As I've mentioned, even if you have a direct contact with the Hiring Manager, you may want to talk to other people first, just to get updated. This is an important step that is often overlooked or ignored. It's almost always a good idea to have a conversation or two with a peer-level non-Hiring Manager before meeting with a Hiring Manager. You never know what you'll discover.

- **People on your Target People list.** Your Target People List should contain people who are not obvious Influencers for a specific target company, but are generally well-connected within your industry or career of interest. They are people who have broad networks and enjoy connecting with and helping others.

- **Everyone else**. Focus on networking with Influencers and target people, and then using everyone else to fill in the gaps. Everyone else is anyone who is not a specific target company Influencer or a person on your Target People List. These are the people you probably already know or people that are referred to you by others you know. This group might include friends, colleagues, former colleagues, and service providers with whom you already have a relationship. *If more than 20% of your meetings are with everyone else, you're not conducting a targeted search.*

Networking Tactics - What to Talk About and Why

Most people don't network effectively as they could when conducting a job search. At the risk of oversimplifying, here's what they do:

- Run through their resume so their networking partner is aware of their experience.
- Ask their networking partner if they know of any good jobs, or anyone who is hiring, or anyone who would be interested in seeing their resume.

Targeted networking takes a different approach and focuses the conversation on your target list of companies and target list of people. It helps move your search forward in a quantifiable way.

Below is an example of a typical interaction using a targeted networking approach. John Doe is meeting a former colleague, Fred Schnoogs, for breakfast to discuss his job search and solicit Fred's assistance. Note how John stays on track with his target list of companies. By doing so, he prompts Fred to think of additional information and contacts that he might otherwise not bring up during the meeting.

> John: Hi Fred, thanks for taking the time to have breakfast with me. As I mentioned in my email, I'm looking for a new job using a targeted approach. The process involves identifying interesting companies for which you'd like to work, and then networking your way into those companies. If you don't mind, I'd like to get your thoughts on some of the companies I'm targeting.

Fred: Sure, John, I'm happy to help with your job search, but I don't know of any companies that are hiring right now.

John: No worries, Fred, I'm just gathering information on my target companies at this point. As you know, I've been running sales for ACME Systems, a $50M company that sells software to large oil & gas companies. I am responsible for hunting and closing many of the company's big multi-million dollar deals. I'm looking for a job running sales for a mid-size software company in Texas.

Here are 10 of the companies that I'm targeting as part of my job search (John shows Fred his target list). Have you heard of XYZ Corp (1st company on the list)? They're a $25M software company in the financial software space. Doug Jones is the CEO, and as I recall, you may have worked with Doug a few years ago. Do you know anything about XYZ and what's going on over there?

Fred: Actually, I do know some of the folks at XYZ, and I just had lunch with Doug last month. They seem to be doing really well. You know, Sally Smith is their VP Sales, and I don't think she's going anywhere else anytime soon.

John: Fred, that's great to hear. Sally certainly has a good reputation. Do you have a sense as what's driving their growth?

Fred: That's a good question. Sounds to me like they've gotten to the point where they are starting to focus on several key vertical markets.

John: That's interesting - a lot of what I did at ACME was help them move from a one-size-fits-all approach to being more vertically oriented. Is there anyone you know at XYZ who you think I should speak with to get an update as to how things are going there?

... and so on for each company on your top 10 target list.

John: Fred, thanks so much for taking a look at my target companies. Your feedback and insights have been very helpful. Now that you know what I'm looking for and the types of companies I'm targeting, are there any other companies you think I should add to my list?

> Fred: Well, now that you mention it, it seems like NewcoSoft and SocialTech should be on your list. NewcoSoft just raised a round of funding, and I heard they are really ramping up their sales efforts. And, SocialTech just hired a new CEO, and I understand she's looking to make some changes.
>
> John: Fred, that's great info. I'll add those companies to my list and check them out. Thanks again for all your help!
>
> Fred: My pleasure, John. This targeted job search approach sounds pretty interesting. Can you point me to their website? I've been thinking maybe it's time for me to start to pop my head up and consider what's next.

Principles of Targeted Networking

Targeted networking takes some practice, but once you've done it a few times, you'll start to get more out of your networking, and it's likely you'll enjoy networking more. Here are a few principles you may find helpful.

- **Be transparent**. Be transparent about why you want to network, and let your network know what you want from them. Be clear about what you're asking for and *not* asking for. Let them know you are using a targeted approach to searching for your next job and that you will be asking them for information on some of your target companies. Tell them you will *not* ask them about hot jobs or which companies are hiring or about specific job openings within their company. If your intentions are clear, and they know of specific jobs for which they think you might be a fit, they will tell you.

- **Leverage your target list.** Let your target list drive the conversation and focus most of your time gathering information about your target companies. Be able to articulate your 30-second elevator pitch if necessary. Inquire about companies that you should add to your target list. If you're networking with the right people, they'll know about companies that you don't, and your target list will help them think of similar companies. Never lead with your resume, but have it available if the opportunity arises to hand it off to someone.

- **Offer to help first.** Ask how you can be helpful and offer your assistance now or in the future. Often, reciprocation will be in the form of what you learned during your job search or the process you followed. Remember, people on average change jobs every four years, and 80% of all people are not happy with their current job.

- **Be efficient.** Don't ask for a meeting when a phone call will do. To be clear, a face-to-face meeting has advantages over a phone call, but be respectful of other people's time, and be respectful of your own time, too. If you meet someone for lunch, you've probably invested at least 2 hours if you include travel time to and from lunch. During that same 2 hours, you could conduct eight 15-minute phone calls. Be thoughtful about whether a call or a meeting is more appropriate. Finding the right job is, to some extent, a numbers game.

- **Ask for contact info and permission to contact.** This is the by far the most avoidable and impactful mistake I see people make. They have a great meeting with their networking partner, and they get a ton of useful info on their target companies and target people. Their networking partner even offers to make an intro to several HMs, Influencers, and target people. How great is that!!! And then the intros never get made. No matter how good people's intentions are about making introductions, they often forget or get sidetracked. The solution is simple: ***get the contact info yourself, and ask for permission to contact directly***. If your networking partners doesn't have the contact info handy, ask for permission to contact the person directly and mention your networking partner's name. If your networking partner declines, don't push, but also realize that at that point, the chances of you actually getting an intro are slim.

2 - Use 30-Day Sprints

I recommend executing your search as a series of 30-day sprints. This provides a great way to focus on your highest-priority companies and reevaluate your approach every 30 days. In addition, it makes it easier to manage your search on a daily basis. By focusing on 10 companies and 10 people within a 30-day window, you're less likely to get distracted or get off track.

Recall the four-step execution process we covered in the last section:

> 1. Find out as much as you can about the company.
> 2. Develop a Point of View (PoV) as to where and how you fit within the company.
> 3. Identify specific Hiring Managers and Influencers.
> 4. Network your way into the company and connect with Hiring Managers.

When we execute an executive search, we use 30-day sprints. Here's how we do it:

- Spend the first week researching target companies, identifying prospective candidates, and researching candidates.
- Solicit the interest of the highest priority candidates aggressively and directly for 2-3 weeks.
    - Use emails as well as phone calls to solicit candidates and give them an easy way to say "no thanks."
    - If they don't respond, try to find a warm intro.
- At the end of 30 days, we reevaluate our strategy and candidate list. We might consider expanding geographically and adding additional candidates.
- Circle back to non-responsive early candidates later in the search and solicit their interest again. Their situation may have changed during the course of the search.

You can apply the same principles to your job search.

- Spend the first week researching target companies, developing your Point of View, and identifying Hiring Managers and Influencers.
- Spend the next 2-3 weeks persistently trying to network your way into a conversation with a Hiring Manager.

- Use phone calls as well as emails. If you don't get a response after a warm intro, 2 calls and 2 emails, move them off your list for now. You may want to circle back to them later in your search.
- Track your progress using the Weekly Scorecard.
- At the end of 30 days, reevaluate your strategy and target lists.

It takes a while to move a company or person through the process, so it's important to have multiple companies and people in process at any given time. You don't need to have exactly 10 companies, but if you have 5, you have too few, and if you have 20, you have too many.

Try to keep all of your companies and people moving forward, even when two or three companies are especially active. It's not unusual to see a flurry of activity around a specific company, and then everything will go silent. And then things will pick up again. And then they'll go silent again. You'll wonder if you did something wrong. Maybe you did, but probably you didn't, and you'll likely never know for sure. Some things you can't control. Rather than focusing too much on the two or three companies that are currently active and moving, try to keep all of your companies and people moving forward. Otherwise, the ups and downs and zigs and zags can drive you crazy.

Here's a simple 30-day sprint plan that you can use to keep your search on track:

- Week 1 - research your target companies, develop a preliminary Point of View, and identify Hiring Managers and Influencers.
- Week 2 - start networking. Send initial email Sunday afternoon/evening, then send 2nd email on Friday. Start scheduling calls/meetings with those who respond.
- Week 3 - continue networking and conduct calls/meetings. Call people from week 2 who did not respond, then send 3rd email on Friday.
- Week 4 - continue networking and conduct calls/meetings. 2nd call to people who have not yet responded. Move people who have not responded off the list for now.

When contacting people who are not responding, my goal is to make sure they are receiving my emails and calls. If they are, and they are not interested in speaking to me, that's fine. A "no" is better than not knowing. When calling people, I prefer to leave a message. Catching a busy executive cold during the day is usually disruptive. Weekends and before/after work hours are good times to call and leave a message.

3 - Track Your Progress

One of the keys to conducting a successful job search is making weekly incremental progress. The Weekly Scorecard at the end of this Module will help you track what's important, quantify your progress, and allow others to help hold you accountable.

> You'll use the Weekly Scorecard every week starting now until you complete your search.

Below are definitions to help you complete your Weekly Scorecard.

Target company definitions:

- **Research completed.** Date on which you completed the initial company research.
- **Orgs/HMs identified.** Date on which you identified organizations of interest to you and the Hiring Managers within those organizations.
- **Warm intro made.** Date on which a warm intro to one of your Hiring Managers was made.
- **Direct contact made.** Date on which you made initial contact (by email or phone) with the Hiring Manager.
- **Call or mtg with HM scheduled.** Date on which you scheduled a call or meeting with the Hiring Manager.
- **Call or mtg with HM completed.** Date on which you held your call or meeting with the Hiring Manager.

Target people definitions:

- **Research completed.** Date on which you completed the initial research on your target person.
- **Orgs/HMs identified.** Date on which you identified organizations and possible Hiring Managers to which your target person is connected.
- **Warm intro made.** Date on which a warm intro to your target person was made.
- **Direct contact made.** Date on which you made initial contact (by email or phone) with the target person.

- **Call or mtg with target person scheduled.** Date on which you scheduled a call or meeting with the target person.
- **Call or mtg with target person completed.** Date on which you held your call or meeting with the target person.

Target Company Research Checklist

Company name: _____

Company website: _____

Size of company: _____

Products and/or services: _____
_____

Industries: _____

Vertical focus: _____

Competitors: _____

- ☐ Video search - YouTube and Vimeo
- ☐ Video search - Google video
- ☐ Video search - Bing video
- ☐ Video search on company name
- ☐ Video search on key executives
- ☐ Search for industry reports or financial analyst reports
- ☐ Google search for PDF and PPT documents

- ☐ Google alert set
- ☐ LinkedIn alert set
- ☐ Facebook friend
- ☐ Follow company on Twitter
- ☐ Follow key executives on Twitter
- ☐ Get high-level organizational structure
- ☐ Run checks on Glassdoor

Possible Hiring Managers:
_____
_____
_____
_____

Possible Influencers:
_____
_____
_____
_____

Preliminary Point of View:
_____
_____
_____

Weekly Scorecard

Top 10 Target Companies (or organizations)	research completed	orgs/HMs identified	warm intro made	direct contact made	call or mtg with HM scheduled	call or mtg with HM completed
1						
2						
3						
4						
5						
6						
7						
8						
9						
10						

Top 10 Target People	research completed	orgs/HMs identified	warm intro made	direct contact made	call or mtg with person scheduled	call or mtg with person completed
1						
2						
3						
4						
5						
6						
7						
8						
9						
10						

Weekly Scorecard

	Top 10 Target Companies (or organizations)	research completed	orgs/HMs identified	warm intro made	direct contact made	call or mtg with HM scheduled	call or mtg with HM completed
1	ACME Widget	12-Jan	12-Jan	15-Jan	15-Jan	15-Jan	21-Feb
2	Industrial Systsms, Inc.	12-Jan	15-Jan	1-Feb	1-Feb		
3	BigCompany.com (NewCo BU)	12-Jan					
4	BigCompany.com (OldCo BU)						
5							
6							
7							
8							
9							
10							

	Top 10 Target People	research completed	orgs/HMs identified	warm intro made	direct contact made	call or mtg with person scheduled	call or mtg with person completed
1	John Doe	12-Jan	12-Jan	15-Jan	15-Jan	15-Jan	21-Feb
2	Jane Doe	12-Jan	15-Jan	1-Feb	1-Feb		
3	Tim Schnoggs	12-Jan					
4							
5							
6							
7							
8							
9							
10							

Notes

Module 6 - Assess

1 - Is the Job a Good Fit for Me?
2 - Am I a Good Fit for the Job?
3 - Job Definition Questions
4 - Job Scorecard
5 - Job Scorecard Example

Module 6 - Assess

Last week you launched your search and began the execution phase. You'll continue executing your search, using 30-day sprints, until you negotiate and close a great opportunity.

As you execute your search and begin to have conversations with Hiring Managers and Influencers, you will enter the **assessment** phase. That's what this Module is about.

When you're talking to Hiring Managers and Influencers, two things are happening:

1. They are assessing you to determine whether or not you are a good fit for the job. This is more commonly known as ***interviewing***, a separate category on Amazon consisting of over 5,200 books.
2. You are assessing the job to determine whether or not it's a good fit for you. I'm not sure I've ever seen a single book written solely on this topic. Typically, the assumption behind interviewing is that you want the job. I won't try to argue that interviewing is unimportant, but this Module will focus more on assessing the job to determine whether or not it's a good fit for you.

Hiring Managers assess you primarily through interviews and reference checks. You'll assess job opportunities primarily through interviews and reference checks as well. To determine whether or not a job is a good fit for you, you'll consider the job itself (the work you'll actually be doing), the job context (how, where, why, and with whom the work gets done), and the market need (compensation economics).

1 - Is the Job a Good Fit for Me?

There's no such thing as a perfect job, but too many people have taken jobs they would **not** have taken had they invested the time to **really** understand the job **before** they accepted an offer. Hardly a day goes by that I don't hear someone say something like, "The job is just not what I thought it was," or "I don't see eye-to-eye with my boss on a number of important issues and values," or "I wish I had taken the time to better understand the culture."

To guide our assessment, we'll use our now familiar 3-circle model as the framework.

Figure 1 - A good job

To understand whether or not a job is a good fit for you, you'll consider:

- How well the **job itself** (the work you'll actually be doing) aligns with your experience (upper right circle).
- How well the **job context** (how, where, why, and with whom the work gets done) aligns with your values (upper left circle).
- How well the **market need** (job compensation) aligns with your economic needs (bottom circle).

1 - Understand the Job Itself

A few years ago, while preparing to recruit a VP Sales for a small company, I had a conversation with the company's CEO. I asked him to share with me his perspective on the company's biggest opportunities and biggest challenges. I asked him to help me understand what he expected the new VP Sales to accomplish during the first 3 months, the first 12 months, and the first 24 months. What types of experiences and abilities would be useful for the new VP Sales to have? Do you want her to focus on building a direct sales force in the US? Or, should the VP Sales be more concerned with developing a channel sales organization in Europe? After getting vague answers to most of my questions, the CEO thought for a minute and said, "I can't tell you exactly what we need, but I'll know it when I see it."

Somehow I doubt it.

This scenario is more common that you might imagine, and it helps to explain why the mis-hire rate in corporate America is between 50 and 75 percent.

> **Searches fail because Hiring Managers don't really know what they're looking for, and they don't really know what they're looking for because they don't understand what the job entails.**

One of the implications of this phenomenon is that a large percentage of jobs for which you interview will *not* be well-defined. In fact, many people I've advised, after learning the technique for better understanding a job, have estimated that over 75% of the jobs for which they interviewed were poorly defined.

> **If you want to find a job that's a good fit for you, it's important to determine whether or not - or how well - you can do the job. To make that assessment, you first have to understand what the job really entails. Since many Hiring Managers aren't very good at job definition, it's your responsibility to ask the right questions to develop your own sense of the job. If you rely on the Hiring Manager to define the job for you, your chances of thoroughly understanding the job will be greatly diminished.**

Develop a Job Scorecard

To understand what a job entails, *your goal should be to define the job in terms of quantifiable, measurable, time-based deliverables*. Geoff Smart, the bestselling author of Who: The A Method for Hiring, uses the term "outcomes" instead of deliverables. Others call them "results" or "success factors."

Whatever you decide to call them, the key point is that you need to develop a picture of what success looks like for a particular job, and the picture should be quantifiable, measurable, and time-based.

Here's an example.

A typical VP Sales job description might say something like:

- Drive revenue growth.
- Hire, train, and manage a world-class sales organization.
- Communicate effectively with other functional leaders.

I hope you agree that the above example does not include quantifiable, measurable, and time-based deliverables.

Here is another example:

- Drive revenue from 15M to 25M in Europe over the next 12 months by developing new partner relationships with 3-4 regional systems integrators.
- Within the next 18 months, transition a geographically-organized North American sales team to a vertically-oriented sales team, focused on financial services and manufacturing.
- Within the first 6 months, build an inside sales team of 10-12 reps focused on driving revenues of the SaaS offering to the SMB market.

The second example provides a much clearer definition of the job and also provides a pretty clear picture of what success looks like.

> Your goal is to work with the Hiring Manager (and his/her team) during the interview process to develop a job definition that looks more like the second example than the first example.

While it's unlikely that you'll be able to completely define the job during the interview process, you can start to quantify many of the specific deliverables and get a much better sense of the job and whether it's a good fit for you.

Whenever I prepare to launch a new search to fill an executive position (typically for a rapidly-growing high-tech startup), I spend a considerable amount of time meeting with my client (the Hiring Manager) and the search committee (other company executives and investors) to define the job. These meetings typically span 1-2 weeks and include one-hour individual meetings with 8-10 executives and investors. ***I spend a lot of time up front trying to understand what the job really entails.***

In fact, the following situation is not that uncommon. I get a call from a prospective client who wants to do an executive search (let's say for a VP of X). We agree to work together and schedule time for meetings to define the job. After a better understanding of what the job really entails, we decide we're not looking for a VP of X, but a VP of Y.

I've developed a list of Job Definition Questions that you can use to guide your conversation with clients to help you better understand the job. I've also developed a Job Scorecard that will help you capture the job definition using quantifiable, measurable, time-based deliverables.

If you find yourself in a situation where you're not getting clear, concise answers to your questions, you can be fairly certain the job you're discussing is not well defined. Another common problem is differing perspectives on job definition. The boss sees the job one way, her peers see it another, and the board sees it still another way.

When you encounter a situation (and you almost certainly will) where the job you're discussing is not well-defined, there are several things you can do:

1. Ignore the importance of a well-defined job, and accept the job if offered.
2. Recognize the importance of a well-defined job, and walk away.
3. Recognize the importance of a well-defined job, and help to define it yourself.

Option three is the most empowering.

If you're interviewing for jobs for which you are well-qualified, then there's a good chance you know as much, if not more, about the job than the Hiring Manager. You are the expert! You are in a position to not only help the Hiring Manager articulate the job definition, but to also influence the job definition itself. This happens all the time on the executive searches I conduct. The best candidates invest the time to understand the job, and then they share their insights with the Hiring Manager regarding the job definition. Sometimes a candidate's feedback will motivate the Hiring Manager to completely rethink and change the job definition. Other times the changes will be more subtle and nuanced. Regardless, the candidates who can help define the job are often finalists for the position.

2 - Understand the Job Context

The job context is more commonly known as corporate culture, and from here on we'll refer to it as such.

Corporate culture is one of those squishy subjects. Virtually everyone agrees that cultural fit is important, but few people agree on what it is. Furthermore, it's a significant challenge to understand and assess the culture of an organization **before** accepting a job.

The goal of this section is to provide you with a framework for cultural assessment that is:

- Easy to understand
- Easy to apply
- Useful, but not necessarily comprehensive
- Based only on information available through the course of a job search

The elements of culture

Here are a few common definitions of corporate culture:

- The collection of beliefs, expectations, and values shared by an organization's members and transmitted from one generation of employees to another. The culture sets norms (rules of conduct) that define acceptable behavior of employees of the organization.
- The set of attitudes, values and behavioral patterns that characterize a particular enterprise.

- The distinctive ethos of an organization that influences the level of formality, loyalty, and general behavior of its employees.

I like to use a more comprehensive definition of culture that includes the following elements:

- Physical context
- Organizational context
- Social context
- Motivational context

Let's deconstruction each of these elements.

- **Physical context.** Do you have a good sense as to where you'll be working? Will you be working in an office? If so, where? How long is the commute? Will you be working in a remote office? If so, how much time will you be expected to spend at the HQ office or other remote offices? Will you be working in a home office? If so, is that appealing to you? How would you describe the office where you'll be working? Open and bright? Closed and dreary? Walled offices? Cubicles? Loud? Quiet? Bright? Dark? Isolated? Open? Chaotic? Serene? A friend of mine was a corporate executive in a large office for many years. It was noisy and chaotic. A couple of years ago he was transferred to a new office that was very quiet and serene. There were only a handful of people on the entire floor. The only noise was from a white noise machine. That would have been nirvana for me. It drove him nuts and became a major source of stress. To what extent is physical context important to you? How does it align with your values?

- **Organization context.** Organizational context is how the company operates and gets things done. It includes several elements:

    o **Work ethic.** The simplest measure of work ethic is average number of hours per week worked. I've worked in companies where 40 hours per week was the norm, and I've worked in companies where 80+ hours per week was the norm. Some companies expect their key employees to be available seven days a week, while others seldom deviate from a 9 to 5, Monday through Friday routine. Is there a formal company policy regarding work hours? Informal policy? When do most people work? Is there an expectation of working evenings? Weekends? While on vacation?

- o **What drives performance.** What drives performance should be addressed at a company as well as at an individual level. Understanding how employees are measured, rewarded, motivated, and promoted will provide insights as to what drives performance within a given company. Is the company obsessed with quarterly financial performance? If so, is there a bias toward revenue growth or profitability? Perhaps the company is less concerned about financial performance and more focused on building a customer base that can be monetized at some future point in time. In some companies, customer service is a key driver. In others, fun, collegiality, and camaraderie play an important role. Understand how and why a company makes money, and you'll understand what drives performance.

- o **Functional orientation.** Many companies tend to be biased towards one of the primary functional organizations: sales, marketing, products, finance, or operations. There are examples of great companies with biases around each of the primary functional areas, so it's not a matter of which is best. It's a matter of which is best for you. An org chart can provide clues to functional bias. In what functional organization do most people reside? Are the company's founders still with the company? If so, what are their functional backgrounds? How do your functional strengths align with the company's functional strengths?

- o **Efficiency and effectiveness.** Some companies are lean and mean, and they function like a well-oiled machine. Others plod along, moving much more slowly and deliberately, but still achieve compelling results. As with other elements of culture, there is no right way or wrong way, but people usually perform better in certain environments. Small, rapidly growing companies are often efficient (they get things done quickly), but they aren't always effective (sometimes they take chances that don't pan out). By contrast, many larger companies are effective, but they may not be as efficient. This cultural element manifests itself vividly when contrasting high-tech startups to larger, more mature companies. Although there are exceptions, small company executives seldom thrive in large companies and vice versa.

- o **Decision making and conflict resolution.** Understanding how decisions are made and how conflicts are resolved is key. Collaborative decision-making organizations present a dramatically different cultural environment than autocratic organizations. Some organizations tend to avoid conflict at almost any cost, while some confront it aggressively and even encourage it. Some companies foster a collaborative decision-making environment combined with conflict avoidance. By contrast, some companies are more autocratic and confrontational.

- o **Clarity of purpose.** Clarity of purpose can refer to the company or to your specific job. In companies with a strong clarity of purpose, everyone understands where the company is going, and everyone understands their role. However, it's not enough for a company to have a well-defined purpose. Its organizations and its individual employees need to have well-define roles and objectives, too. I often encounter executives who are frustrated because they don't understand exactly what their job entails, or because their job definition changes frequently.

- **Social context.** Social context includes work style, the people, community, trust, and sense of belonging. Do people work alone or in teams? Are teams fluid and self-organizing or more permanent and rigid. How would you describe the people who work for the company? Are they fun? Are they serious? Are they energized? Stressed? Do people eat lunch together? Is there a large common area? Are there after-hours events? Do people spend time together outside of work? Is there a sense of connectedness across organizations? Or are organizations relatively isolated? Do people trust one another? Do they jump in to cover someone's back when appropriate?

- **Motivational context.** Motivational context addresses the dominant work motivations across the company. Are most people there for the money? Are they "coin operated?" Are most people there for intrinsic reasons, such as meaning or mission? How are people rewarded? Compensated? Acknowledged? Promoted? Evaluated? Disciplined? Hired? Fired? To what extent are people provided autonomy in their work? To what extent is learning and growth supported? To what extent are mistakes tolerated or encouraged? What do people take pride in? To what extent do people believe in the mission or purpose of the company? How do the motivations of employees within the company align with your own motivations and values?

Assessing Culture

While it's unlikely you are going to find a culture that fits perfectly with your style and values, it's useful to try to understand as much as you can about a company's culture during the interview process. To do so, you'll need to rely primarily on the following three techniques:

- **Q&A during interviews.** Although it may seem obvious to ask about culture during interviews, not everyone does it. When posing cultural questions, you're looking for *consistent answers* across the organization, so ask everyone about the cultural elements that are important to you. Ask specific questions regarding the cultural framework elements above (e.g., how are decisions made?) as well as open-ended questions (e.g., what's your culture like?). In many companies, your prospective boss will determine many of the elements of culture. Make sure his/her perspectives are in sync with other team members' perspectives. If you're interviewing for a job that has a significant cross-functional component, make sure you speak directly with cross-functional peers during the interviews.

- **Research and observation.** Research the backgrounds of the people you meet during the interview process. Where have they previously worked and what were the cultures of these companies? Are they job-hoppers, or do they tend to stay in one company for a long time? Notice who participates in the interview process and how much time each person is allocated. Do you spend two hours with your prospective boss, but only 30 minutes with your prospective peers and subordinates? Are there people that appear to be intentionally excluded from the interview process? Pay attention to what's going on in the office. Did you show up at 9am and were the first one to arrive? Does everyone leave for lunch, or do most people skip lunch or eat at their desks? Is the office open and accessible or secluded and closed? There are cultural clues everywhere if you are observant. If you haven't already done so, use Glassdoor.com to gain an insider's perspective. Take strong negative feedback (often from former employees) with a grain of salt, but use the feedback to guide questioning during interviews.

- **Reverse reference checks.** This point probably deserves a separate section or perhaps even a separate book! ***Reverse reference checks are by far the most important and revealing technique and by far the least used technique to evaluate corporate culture.*** Way too many executives fail to conduct reverse reference checks on their prospective boss, and way too many regret it. Always, always, always conduct reverse reference checks. Always, always, always do reverse reference checks on your prospective boss. I suggest doing at least three. Talk to former employees if you can find them, but don't be afraid to ask for references as well. If you speak to former employees who may have been asked to leave, be aware of possible sour grapes. Unless you're interviewing for a newly-created position, someone has already held this job in this company. Find out who it was, and talk to them.

Often culture varies, sometimes significantly, within organizations in a given company. Any organization, regardless of its size, is likely to have a distinct culture. Your work group will have its own culture, your business unit will have its own culture, and the entire company will have its own culture. **Arguably the most relevant aspect of culture is that created by your direct supervisor.** When assessing cultural fit, you'll want to make sure you consider how culture varies across the company and how the culture defined by your boss is similar or different.

One final thought. Some folks are just naturally more flexible and adaptable than others, and they can adjust to almost any cultural environment. However, for most people, there will be some elements of culture that are important and worth understanding while assessing fit.

3 - Understand the Market Need

Understanding the market need during the assessment phase means getting a sense as to whether or not you're in the ballpark on compensation.

Granted, it's unlikely you'll completely understand the compensation until you receive a formal offer, but it's almost always possible (and advisable) to get a general sense of compensation as you're going through the assessment phase.

Here's what I suggest. After a couple of interactions with the Hiring Manager, if things seem to be going well, ask the Hiring Manager what the compensation parameters are for the job. If you don't get an answer, you can try a couple of things. You can suggest a compensation range that you think is appropriate for the job, and see how the Hiring Manager reacts. Or, you can share your current and compensation history with the Hiring Manager.

You don't want to negotiate at this point. Your best leverage point for negotiation is right after you receive a formal offer and before you accept the job. At this point, you just want to make sure you're directionally correct.

4 - How Good of a Fit is Good Enough?

One of my recruiting clients once posed the following question.

If we keep working on the search for three more months, what is the chance we're going to find a candidate who is better than the top candidate we have now?

It's basically the same question that you'll ask yourself when assessing a specific opportunity.

> If I keep working on my job search for three more months, what is the chance I'm going to find a job that's better than this job?

At the end of the day, determining whether or not a job is a good fit is a subjective decision, but here are three things that will help you answer the question:

- **An informed perspective.** In the Introduction, I suggested you give yourself 6 months of runway to conduct a job search. One of the main reasons you need 6 months is because it takes time to develop an informed perspective on the market. Are you still discovering interesting new companies to add to your target list? Are you still meeting interesting new people that are in your ecosystem of interest? If so, then you may need more time. When you start hearing about the same companies and getting introduced to the same people, you probably have as informed a perspective on the market as you're going to get.

- **Enough information.** You'll never have all of the information, but there's an opportunity for most people to collect a lot more information than they do. Have you run all the traps and followed all the steps? Or, did you skip a few steps (like reverse reference checks on your boss)? Were you transparent during the interview process? Transparency increases the chances that the hiring company will be able to assess your fit for the job. Did the job definition become more focused as the process progressed? While the job may never be completely defined, was the Hiring Manager able to provide increasing detail as the interviews progressed? Was their assessment process thorough and relevant? Companies and Hiring Managers who know what they're looking for tend to do a better job of interviewing and assessment. Cursory or superficial interviews should be a red flag. What else do you need to know to understand the job? Who else do you need to meet with or talk to, or what additional information do you need? The best Hiring Managers will pose these questions to you before extending an offer. What else do you need to know to understand the culture? Who else do you need to meet with or talk to, or what additional information do you need? Did you spend time on Glassdoor? Did you speak to former employees?

- **Consideration of your limitations.** How's your financial situation? For some people, economic reality overrides the elements of fit. What's your level of anxiety over the job search process? Let's face it, finding a job can be emotionally draining and fraught with anxiety, even for senior executives with successful careers and significant wealth. If you're tired of searching and just ready to get back to work, you should factor this into your assessment. Some people enjoy the job search process. Others want it to be over as soon as possible.

2 - Am I a Good Fit for the Job?

The process of the Hiring Manager determining whether or not you are a good fit for the job is commonly known as *interviewing*.

> Interviewing is complex, but conceptually it's pretty simple. Interviewing is about understanding what the job **really** entails, and then communicating your relevant experience and accomplishments to the Hiring Manager.

That's one of the main reasons why it's so important to understand the job before trying to sell yourself. Candidates who start selling themselves prematurely often come across as desperate. They focus on accomplishments that may be irrelevant or superficial. The best candidates are intrigued, but somewhat skeptical. They want to understand the details of the job before they start selling themselves. Yes, it's to your advantage to stay positive and show interest, but you don't want to oversell yourself, especially before understanding the details of the job.

During the course of my experience as a recruiter, I've conducted thousands of executive interviews. I've discussed thousands more conducted by my clients, typically CEOs and board members. In addition, every time I meet with a prospective client, I'm being interviewed myself to potentially conduct a search. So I interview hundreds of executives every year, but I'm also interviewed 20-30 times every year.

This Module on interviewing is not intended to be remedial. Most managers and executives have mastered the basics of interviewing. My intent is to remind and provide a holistic perspective on contemporary interviewing.

My formula for successful interviewing has four steps:

- Refresh your memory
- Prepare
- Interview
- Manage the process

1 - Refresh Your Memory

Prior to each interview, it's good practice to refresh your memory on relevant experiences and accomplishments that might come up in the interview. If you want to be able to quickly recall and articulate those experiences and accomplishments, it's easier if they're fresh in your mind.

The best way to do this is to review your answers to the Career Inventory Exercise. The Career Inventory Exercise is based on an interview approach advocated by Dr. Bradford Smart in his best-selling book entitled Topgrading. Topgrading extols the virtues of using a Chronological In-Depth Structured (CIDS) approach to interviewing and assessment. It is a very thorough approach to assessment, and it's becoming more popular. Regardless of whether or not you are given a CIDS-type interview, reviewing your Career Inventory answers is still a great way to prepare.

> If you're apprehensive about interviewing, or it's been awhile since you've interviewed for a job, consider practicing mock interviews with a trusted friend or colleague. A simple but effective approach is to have the interviewer use the Career Inventory questions as a template.

2 - Prepare

Interview research should consist of more than perusing a company website. ***A well-prepared candidate will take a more comprehensive approach that includes not only the company, but also the industry, the people, and the job.*** The more senior and experienced you are, the more in-depth your research and preparation needs to be.

To be as prepared as possible, I suggest the following:

- **Research the company thoroughly using the Job Definition Questions from the last Module as a guideline.** The initial company research you conducted focused getting an overall sense of the company, its size, the industry in which it competes, high-level financial data, and organizational structure. In preparing for an interview with a Hiring Manager, you'll want to dive deeper. Use the list of Job Definition Questions from the last Module to try to find as many answers as you can through research. The questions are included at the end of this Module as well.

- **Conduct a couple of blind references.** If you've followed the process up to this point, you may have already spoken to a couple of Influencers related to your target company. Now might be a good time to circle back to those folks and dig a little deeper. You might approach one of the influencers and say, "Thanks in part to our call a couple of weeks ago, I am meeting with Sally Smith at ACME to discuss a sales leadership position. What can you tell me about Sally? What do you know about the sales team at ACME?" If you have the opportunity to ask more in-depth questions, consider these. What are Sally's strengths? What is she really good at? What is she not so good at? Who are her critics at ACME? What do her critics say about her? How would you describe Sally's management style? What types of people tend to work best with her?

- **Look for common points of interest to create a more personal conversation with the Hiring Manager.** Common interests, common people, especially those who might act as positive references for you.

Be prepared to ask insightful questions. More and more of my clients are turning the tables and starting the interview by asking, "What questions do you have for me?" They believe, as do I, that you can learn a lot by the types of questions a candidate asks.

One more point - if you're not willing to do the research, don't take the interview. It makes you look bad. I interview too many execs who ask superficial questions they could have figured out by spending 10 minutes on the company's website. Your behavior during the interview process is assumed to be a proxy for how you'll behave on the job.

3 - Interview

Here are my favorite interviewing tips and tricks. While some may seem obvious or overly tactical, many people will benefit by reviewing these before important interviews.

- **Get a name and number to call in advance in case you are running late.** Sometimes stuff happens, and you end up running late. If it looks like you may be more than a couple of minutes late, call the Hiring Manager (or assistant) and let them know you're running late.

- **Provide transparency into yourself and experiences.** While this may seem intuitive, it's not the approach most people take. Most people temper their answers to questions with a bias towards what they think the interviewer wants to hear. The better you know yourself - your strengths, weaknesses, passions, etc. - the better your chances of finding a rewarding job. A good rule of thumb to follow: give clear, concise, direct answers to questions, and back up your answers with specific examples.

- **Think out loud.** In the spirit of providing transparency, thinking out loud will help the interviewer gain insights into how you think as well as how you structure and solve problems. If someone asks you what time it is, don't tell them how to build a clock, but if someone asks you how to build a clock, you're probably better off thinking out loud.

- **Listen carefully to questions to infer job responsibilities.** The questions you are asked during an interview will often give you more clarity into the job than the job spec or anything the Hiring Manager says directly. This is an important point, so I am going to repeat it! The questions you are asked during an interview will often give you more clarity into the job than the job spec. For example, if you are interviewing for a senior marketing role, and most of the questions are about your sales experience, the marketing role you're envisioning may turn out to be more of a sales position. Job specs are often written as "sell sheets" or to describe the job under ideal conditions.

- **Drop some names.** I recommend dropping the names of your former bosses and people you've worked with who know you well. Check LinkedIn to see if you share any common connections with the Hiring Manager. If those common connections know you well, mention them to the interviewer. Resist the temptation to drop the names of prominent people who may know you, but don't know you well enough to provide credible first-hand feedback.

- **Highlight learnings, not failures.** Chances are you've endured some failures or setbacks along the way. Virtually *every* senior executive I've interviewed has had his/her share of challenges. The successful ones tend to learn and move on, while the unsuccessful ones tend to make excuses and dwell. When asked about failures, whether it's why you were let go or why you missed your sales quota or why you didn't get along with the CFO, it's usually best to answer the question in the context of what you learned from the experience.

4 - Manage the Process

You may not be able to **control** the interview process, but you can **understand** and possibly **influence** the process. It's incumbent upon you to "qualify yourself" as a candidate - to understand the interview process, where things stand, next steps in the process, your position vis-a-vis other candidates, etc. Think like a sales exec who is trying to qualify her pipeline of prospects. Be sure to identify the decision maker and to clarify the timeline on next steps and when the final decision will be made. Ask questions so that you can assess your chances of receiving an offer of employment. How many other candidates are being considered? What will be the criteria for selecting the final candidate? What are the possible objections regarding your candidacy?

Types of Interview Questions

Interview questions almost always fall into one of the following categories:

- **Simple factual questions.** These types of questions include job title verification, dates of employment, education and degrees, dates of employment, etc.

- **Industry knowledge questions.** Most senior positions require some knowledge of the industry in which the company competes.

- **Functional knowledge questions.** If you're interviewing for a functional role (sales, marketing, finance, etc.), it's likely you'll get questions that test your knowledge and experience in that specific functional area.

- **Experiential questions.** Experiential questions are usually focused on role and responsibilities and what you accomplished in a given job. The best answers are usually crisp and concise, and supported with specific examples.

- **Behavioral questions.** Focuses on the how of what you've accomplished, as well as the what. Behavioral questions usually take the form of "tell me about a time when you did XYZ" or , "Give me a specific example of how you did XYZ." The rationale behind behavioral questions is that past behaviors drive future behaviors. Behavioral interview questions often form the basis of executive interviews.

- **Company questions.** Many Hiring Managers want to make sure you've taken the time to understand the company for which they work.

- **Brain teasers.** An example of this type of question includes, "How many gas stations are there in Europe?" or "How much does a 747 weigh?" Their purpose is to evaluate your IQ and problem structuring/solving abilities. Brain teasers seem to be more prevalent with junior executives, but occasionally I'll see them used with more senior executives. Other examples of brain teasers include, "Estimate the number of piano tuners in the US" or "What would happen if the price of oil went to zero?" With most brain teasers, the interviewer is *not* looking for the correct answer as much as she is trying to get a sense of how you think, structure problems, and solve problems. As such, it's always best to think out loud when answering these types of questions.

- **Case interviews.** In a typical case interview, you are presented with a hypothetical situation or business case to resolve. Often the interviewer pulls from her own background to create a case to present to you. Case interviews are popular with management consulting firms, investment banks, and some technology companies. At the executive level, you might be given a "real-life" case instead of a hypothetical situation. An example might be, "Our company is committed to 20% growth for next year. How would you go about formulating a sales strategy that would allow us to hit that target?" As with brain teasers, the interviewer is likely trying to get a sense of how you think, structure problems, and solve problems, so it's best to think out loud.

- **The 90-day plan.** I'm starting to see this type of interview question more frequently at the executive level. The typical scenario is that you're asked to put together a 90-day plan (or 30-day plan or 6-month plan) for the job for which you are interviewing. In my experience, this is usually less of a formal plan or presentation and more of a dialogue about what you would do if given the job. The interview may last 1-2 hours and sometimes involves using a whiteboard to sketch ideas. Sometimes candidates are given supporting data (such as company financials) a few days in advance of the interview and asked to use the data when developing their plan.

- **Psychometric assessments.** According to Wikipedia, Psychometrics is the field of study concerned with the theory and technique of psychological measurement, which includes the measurement of knowledge, abilities, attitudes, personality traits, and educational measurement. Pragmatically, psychometric tests typically include IQ tests and personality tests. For many years, it was believed that preparation for psychometric tests was useless. More recently, it has been shown that preparation can be useful. There are a myriad of good websites and test prep services that you may find useful if you are asked to take psychometric tests. Here are a couple of sites that offer free sample tests: Institute of Psychometric Coaching, Psychometric Success.

3 - Job Definition Questions

Industry questions
- What are the three most important trends shaping the industry today?
- How fast is the industry growing?
- Who is disrupting the industry and how?
- Who are your main competitors?
- How are you positioned vis-a-vis your main competitors?
- Do you have any industry analyst or financial analyst reports that you can share with me?

Company, organization, and job questions
- With regards to the company, organization, or job in question, what's working well today?
- With regards to the company, organization, or job in question, what's not working so well today?
- What are the three biggest opportunities for
    - the company
    - the business unit, division, or group, etc.
    - this specific job
- For each of the biggest opportunities, what must:
    - the company do to capitalize on the opportunity?
    - the business unit, division, or group, etc. do to capitalize on the opportunity?
    - the person who gets this job do to capitalize on the opportunity?
- What are the three biggest challenges for
    - the company
    - the business unit, division, or group, etc.
    - the person who gets this job
- For each of the biggest challenges, what must:
    - the company do to overcome the challenge?
    - the business unit, division, or group, etc. do to overcome the challenge?
    - the person who gets this job do to overcome the challenge?
- If the person hired is successful in this role, what will he/she have accomplished over the next

- o 6 months,
- o 12 months,
- o 24 months,
- o 36 months?
- If this job existed before,
  - o What did the previous employee do well?
  - o What did the previous employee not do so well?
- What are the three most important constituencies (other internal groups or organizations, customers, external groups or organizations, shareholders, etc.) to which this job interfaces?
- Vis-à-vis this position,
  - o What will this person's boss do?
  - o What will this person's peers do?
  - o What will this person's subordinates do?

Sales questions
- What is the current sales model?
- How large is the current sales staff, including SEs, sales ops, etc.?
- What is the average deal size?
- What is the pricing model?
- What are the various components of revenue?
- Can you share a list of current customers?
- Who are your reference customers?
- What is the compensation structure for sales reps?
- What is the sales rep turnover rate?
- What is the profile of leading sales rep?
- Who is the customer/decision maker?
- What is the average sales cycle time?

Product Development questions
- How is product differentiated vs. competitors' products?
- What is the value proposition?
- How long is the installation/integration cycle?
- What new products are in development?
- Is there a formal product management process in place? If so, who owns it?
- Have there been any patents awarded or filed?

Marketing questions
- What is the company's current positioning?
- Can you share copies of industry/competitive reports?
- Can you share copies of any whitepapers?
- Can you share copies of any published articles?
- What are the primary events, seminars, and conferences?
- What are the primary industry associations?
- What are the primary industry publications, websites, trade rags, etc.
- What is the current year marketing budget?
- How are marketing dollars spent?
- How are leads generated?

Finance questions (for private companies)
- What is the company's funding history, including debt?
- Can you share with me the high-level capital structure?
- How much cash is in the bank?
- What is the monthly net burn rate?
- Are there any preference multiples on invested capital?
- What was the company's most recent valuation?
- Can you share with me the company's trailing two years EBITDA and cash flow?
- Can you share with me the company's projected revenue for the next two years?
- What are the company's likely exit options and timing?
- Do you anticipate additional funding prior to exit?

Job Scorecard

Job Title: _____ Reports to: _____

Direct Reports: _____

Total Staff: _____

Industry: _____ Industry Segment: _____

Function: _____ Function Segment: _____

Vertical Orientation: _____

Size of Company: _____ Growth Rate: _____

Is this a new position or a replacement position? _____

If new position, what's driving its creation? _____

If replacement position, what happened to the person who is being replaced? _____

Position Charter: _____
_____
_____

Quantifiable, measurable, time-based deliverable #1:
_____
_____

Quantifiable, measurable, time-based deliverable #2:
_____
_____

Quantifiable, measurable, time-based deliverable #3:
_____
_____

Job Scorecard Example

Job Title: Vice President of Sales   Reports to: CEO

Direct Reports: Sales Director West, Sales Director East, Sales Manager Europe, Inside Sales Manager

Total Staff: 25

Industry: Software   Industry Segment: SaaS CRM software

Function: Sales   Function Segment: Sales

Vertical Orientation: Mostly large financial services and manufacturing companies

Size of Company: 50M revenue   Growth Rate: 45% annually

Is this a new position or a replacement position?   replacement

If new position, what's driving its creation?   NA

If replacement position, what happened to the person who is being replaced?   terminated

Position Charter:

Triple revenue over three years through European expansion, focus on vertical markets, and inside sales.

Quantifiable, measurable, time-based deliverable #1:

Drive revenue from 15M to 25M in Europe over the next 12 months by developing new partner relationship with 3-4 regional systems integrators.

Quantifiable, measurable, time-based deliverable #2:

Within the next 18 months, transition a geographically-organized North American sales team to a vertically-oriented sales team, focused on financial services and manufacturing.

Quantifiable, measurable, time-based deliverable #3:

Within the first 6 months, build an inside sales team of 10-12 reps focused on driving revenues of the SaaS offering in the SMB market.

Notes

Module 7 - Negotiate and Close

1 - Pre-Negotiation Checklist
2 - Negotiation Principles
3 - Lessons from the Trenches
4 - Further Reading
5 - Job Offer Checklist
6 - Exercise

Module 7 - Negotiate and Close

When you find a job that's a good fit, you'll negotiate and close the deal. You'll use the pre-negotiation checklist to prepare before you start to negotiate. After you receive an offer, you'll use the job offer checklist as a guideline while reviewing. You'll also use my negotiation principles and lessons learned to help keep things on track and optimize the chances of a favorable outcome.

Sometimes, during the heat of negotiation, we lose site of the bigger picture. We become consumed by the negotiation, and it becomes a win/lose competition focused on money. Now is a good time to pause and revisit what's really important to you. To be clear, all else being equal, more money is usually better than less money. But it's seldom the case that all else is equal.

If you haven't already done so, review your career values from the Career Success Exercise from Module 2. What were your ten most important career values? Did you have any non-negotiable values? If so, what were they?

> **Realize that during the negotiation phase of the process, your tendency will be to minimize the importance of dissatisfiers, overvalue extrinsic rewards, and undervalue intrinsic rewards.**

Review your Target Job Profile from Module 3 as well. Have you stayed true to your profile? How well does the job you're negotiating conform to your target? How do you justify the variances?

> *You can negotiate like a pro and still lose out if the negotiation you're in is the wrong one. Ultimately, your satisfaction hinges less on getting the negotiation right and more on getting the job right. Experience and research demonstrate that the industry and function in which you choose to work, your career trajectory, and the day-to-day influences on you (such as bosses and coworkers) can be vastly more important to satisfaction than the particulars of an offer.*
>
> Deepak Malhotra - **Professor, Harvard Business School and author of** Negotiation Genius

As you enter the negotiation and close phase, I invite you to consider this question:

> Do you really want this job?

There are three possible answers.

1) **You want the job.** If you want the job, that's great. It's time to try to negotiate a deal you find compelling. This Module should be helpful.
2) **You don't want the job.** Many people negotiate jobs they don't want. Maybe you're trying to establish your market value, or perhaps you want to use an offer as leverage to negotiate a raise with your current company. Ethically, I think you're on thin ice here, but ultimately it's your decision.
3) **You're unsure whether or not you want the job.** If you're unsure as to whether or not you want the job, I suggest you return to Module 6 on assessment. What else do you need to know about the job, the company, or the culture to make a decision? There is still time to try to get more information and eliminate, or at least reduce, the uncertainty.

Assuming you want the job, this Module should help you negotiate and close a solid offer.

1 - Pre-Negotiation Checklist

When you first receive an offer of employment, you may be tempted to start negotiating right away. Instead, I suggest the following steps *before* you initiate negotiations:

- Review the offer yourself
- Review the offer with someone more knowledgeable if possible
- Clarify the offer with the Hiring Manager
- Have an attorney review the offer
- Collect compensation information
- Determine BATNAs (Best Alternative to Negotiated Agreement)
- Determine the decision maker
- Determine timing
- Review your definition of career success
- Review your target job profile

Let's consider each of the above pre-negotiation steps in more detail.

- **Review the offer yourself.** Depending on the employer, the seniority of the role, and the complexity of the offer, you may receive anything from a one-page informal offer letter to a twenty-page formal employment agreement with references to other legal documents. As a first step, you can use the Job Offer Checklist at the end of this lesson to make sure the main components of the offer have been included.

- **Review the offer with someone more knowledgeable if possible.** If you know someone who has more experience than you with similar types of offers, this would be a great time to solicit their input.

- **Clarify the offer with the Hiring Manager.** You may receive an initial offer verbally or in writing. Regardless, the first thing to do is to try to understand all the elements of the offer. Get clarification on all elements of compensation, job definition, and any other loose ends (relocation allowance, paid vacation, benefits, etc.). *Don't negotiate, don't judge, don't get emotional. Just clarify.*

- **Have an attorney review the offer.** Depending on your seniority and the complexity of the offer, you may want to get an attorney involved at this point. Take responsibility for developing an agreement that's fair and as unambiguous as possible. I suggest using an attorney who will edit and clarify. Be cautious of using an attorney who wants to rewrite substantive sections of the agreement. Overly aggressive editing can set the stage for an adversarial negotiation, which can jeopardize the negotiation and result in an unnecessary expense to you.

- **Collect compensation information.** There are a number of different data points that can be collected to develop a sense of market compensation:

    - Your compensation history
    - Your current compensation
    - Monetary impact of leaving your current job (realized but unpaid bonuses, unvested options, exercising options, etc.)
    - Compensation survey data
    - Peer compensation in similar roles in similar companies in same geographic area
    - Peer compensation within the company extending the offer
    - Competing offers

    Share your data points, and ask them to share theirs. Gather as much factual information as you can. With a little effort, you should be able to collect more compensation data than the average Hiring Manager. While it's possible that compensation data may not significantly influence the negotiation, I've seen many situations when it was a determining factor. Better to be prepared than not.

    For super complex offers, consider building a cash flow model that shows timing and magnitude of cash flows. Sharing the cash flow model with the Hiring Manager can lead to clarification.

- **Determine and clarify BATNAs.** Your BATNA is your Best Alternative to a Negotiated Agreement. It's your Plan B. Maybe even your Plan C. Many experts argue that having a well-defined fallback position puts you in the best position to negotiate your best deal. ***Make sure you not only determine your BATNAs, but you also clarify them.*** Do you have a competing offer on the table? If so, have you clarified all of the terms of that offer, or are there still some uncertainties? People are too often vague about their BATNAs, which leads them to overestimate the strength of their positions.

It's also worth trying to understand the company's BATNA. Does the company have several other qualified candidates in the pipeline in case they can't come to terms with you? Or, are you the only candidate? How long has the company been trying to fill this position? Is this a new position or a backfill? How critical is this position to the strategic direction of the company?

- **Determine the decision maker.** The Hiring Manager is usually the decision maker, but not always. Occasionally, they'll be a key influencer behind the scenes that you may need to involve. Perhaps the Hiring Manager's boss is pushing hard for lower base salary. Maybe a board member has an issue with the amount of equity being offered.

- **Determine timing.** By when does the company want a response? It's best to ask and not make assumptions. They might be thinking you'll respond immediately, and you might be thinking you've got two weeks. Misaligned expectations can undermine the negotiation. If they want a quick response, just ask for more time, but be prepared to have a couple of good reasons. Having an attorney or third party review an offer will often buy you at least a week.

Once you've completed the above preparation steps, you'll be in a much better position to negotiate effectively.

2 - Negotiation Principles

I've developed a set of principles to help guide you through the negotiation process.

- **Don't take shortcuts.** Receiving an offer from a company in which you're interested is pretty exciting! But exciting is a poor excuse for neglecting reverse reference checks, shortcutting due diligence, and ignoring cautionary flags. Stay true to the process: *this is the worst time to take a shortcut*.

- **Choreograph the close.** For managers and executives, the negotiation phase may last one to four weeks or more. While it may not be possible for you to completely control the timing and duration, it most cases it's possible to influence the pace. If this is the job you want, and the deal is strong, you may want to push the pace and get it done. As an investment banker once said, "The only things that can happen between the time a deal is agreed upon and formally consummated are all bad." However, in this scenario, I recommend *not* rushing the process unnecessarily. It's likely you'll learn as much about the company and your new boss during this final phase as you have up to this point. You'll need to balance your desire to get the deal closed with new information you'll glean during this final phase. If, by contrast, you have another opportunity in your pipeline that has the potential to be an even better job for you (or you want to make sure you have a fallback job lined up), you may be motivated to try to slow the pace a bit. In the perfect world, you'll be able to "choreograph the close," and you'll approach the home stretch of your search with two or three solid opportunities that reach the offer stage at roughly the same time. One word of caution. If you're trying to slow the pace, make sure you're still being responsive, or you run the risk of losing favor with the company.

- **Negotiate the job as well as the compensation.** Most people focus on negotiating compensation, but negotiating job definition can sometimes be more important and impactful. For example, it's not uncommon for the job definition to change during the course of interviews and negotiation. Often, the role expands and new responsibilities are included. In this scenario, clarifying and reaching mutual agreement on the expanded job definition puts you in a position to negotiate for higher compensation than what the original job entailed. Another common scenario is the use of performance-based compensation, where part of your compensation is tied to your individual performance, often in the form of pre-determined metrics. These pre-determined metrics essentially define your job. Negotiating and agreeing on the proper metrics can have a significant impact on compensation.

- **Negotiate all compensation elements, not just base and bonus.** Don't just focus on negotiating the cash compensation aspects of an offer (or in some cases cash and equity). There may be other elements of the job that are important to negotiate. It's often the case that there is less flexibility around cash compensation and more flexibility around these other elements. Examples of non-cash compensation elements may include:

    o Annual bonus structure (capped, uncapped, accelerators, performance criteria, guarantees, etc.)
    o Long-term incentives
    o Benefits
    o Pre-negotiated bump in compensation or pre-negotiated promotion
    o Signing bonus
    o Vacation
    o Severance
    o Vesting schedule and/or accelerated vesting
    o Change of control provisions
    o Carve out provisions
    o Relocation expenses (including temporary living and real estate expenses)

- **Contemplate compensation in the context of some estimated period of time.** It's important to understand the temporal aspects of your employment agreement. People are changing jobs with increasing frequency, so it's worth considering how long you expect to be in the job. Be cognizant of "backend-loaded" agreements, where much of the wealth creation occurs only after several years of employment. In the case of equity, understand vesting schedules and the implications of departure. One of the best ways to understand a complex compensation agreement is to model compensation cash flows over some period of time and share with the company to gain concurrence.

- **Focus on improving, or at least not damaging, the relationship with your new employer.** A great article that builds upon this idea is Getting Past Yes: Negotiating as if Implementation Mattered. The author, Danny Ertel, postulates that sometimes negotiators focus too much on closing the deal and squeezing the best terms out of one another and not enough on the post-deal relationship. This is especially true when negotiating a job offer, where negotiating aggressively with your new boss can have significant ramifications. If you want a great job, it is important to negotiate a fair deal and get off on the right foot.

- **Negotiate your best deal before you start the job.** This probably seems obvious, but I see too many jobs that are accepted with loose ends that the parties intend to "iron out" later. You'll never have more negotiating leverage than you do **before** you start the job, so I suggest nailing down everything before accepting.

- **If negotiations stall, reiterate your value.** If negotiations stall, try taking a step back from the offer elements that are sticking points, and reiterate your value to the company. No one cares about your mortgage or your car payments, but it's likely they care about how much impact you can have in the job.

    - Be specific about how you can help the company.
    - Develop and present a 3-month plan with quantifiable results.
    - Clarify your experiences and strengths that are relevant to the position.
    - Clarify your record of performance and accomplishments.
    - Make sure the company is speaking to your references, and offer to provide more references if there are areas the company wants to probe further.

- **Always be responsive, remain excited, and create a positive perspective.** I've seen firsthand how a candidate's less-than-excited attitude or lack of responsiveness can negatively impact negotiations. It's easy for a Hiring Manager to assume the candidate may not really want the job, and, as a result, the candidate may lose some leverage. Always be responsive, but don't appear desperate. Even if you need to walk away from the deal, do so in a way that leaves the door open to future negotiations.

3 - Lessons from the Trenches

As a recruiter, I conduct 10 to 15 searches per year. This means I basically negotiate my salary 10 to 15 times per year. Here are some lessons I've learned the hard way.

- **Be wary of those who pay over market.** Those who pay over market usually do so for a reason, and it's not because they are just naturally generous. I had a client once who bragged about how well he paid recruiters. I submitted a contract with a fee well above my standard fee. They didn't balk. As the search progressed, I learned why; most recruiters didn't want to work with them regardless of how much they paid.

- **Be wary of those who pay under market.** From time to time, I've agreed to do searches for clients who paid me under market. The reasons usually involved a variation of one of the following: a passionate CEO whose vision to change the world was compelling, a struggling company that just needed one or two more deals to turn the corner, a CEO who had been mistreated by a prior recruiter and was skeptical. None of my "under market" clients were good clients. My best clients compensate me fairly for my efforts.

- **Don't negotiate with an intermediary.** My clients are typically either CEOs or investors. From time to time, an intermediary (such as a CFO, attorney or VP HR) is inserted into the process to negotiate and finalize the contract. Here's what I've learned. The insertion of an intermediary into the process is an indication that my client (the CEO or investor) wants to work with me. If I hold my ground, eventually the CEO/investor will start pressuring the intermediary to get the deal done. It's usually just a matter of being patient.

- **Ask why before negotiating.** When my contract comes back full of changes, the first thing I do is schedule a call to walk through the agreement. I ask the client to clarify the change, and then I inquire as to the motivation behind the change (often, it's not what I would have guessed). Having a client explain to me why a 40% discount is justified can be an enlightening experience for the client, sometimes alleviating the need to negotiate.

- **The negotiation process is a great proxy for what it's going to be like working with the company.** I now pay close attention to the negotiation process. Does my client delegate the negotiating? Is she responsive? Does she take the negotiation personally? Is she always too busy to get the deal done? Is her style more objective or more emotional? Does she always seem hurried and stressed or calm and in control? Does she always need to be right? Does she blame external factors (her boss, corporate policies, budget constraints, etc.) for not being able to consummate the deal? Do I trust her? Does she trust me?

- **Mis-aligned interests are showstoppers.** My clients sometimes try to change the parameters of my standard agreement in a way that mis-aligns our incentives. They want to make our contract contingent, or they want to source their own candidates and run a parallel process. While these may seem like good ideas, they mis-align our incentives in a way that can adversely impact the outcome. If, after explaining to the client how their suggested changes are not in their own best interest, they insist on an agreement with mis-aligned incentives, I walk away.

- **Always stay positive.** You might be thinking that there's no way that the deal is going to get done, but the last thing you should do is project frustration. Regardless of how big the gap, remain positive and keep negotiating. If the client thinks the deal is going to get done, they are less likely to seek alternatives. If the client thinks the deal won't get done, they are going to start investing more energy in Plan B.

4 - Further Reading

For those of you interested in a deeper understanding of negotiation, I suggest the following books.

- Getting to Yes: Negotiating Agreement Without Giving In by Fisher and Ury.
- In Business As in Life, You Don't Get What You Deserve, You Get What You Negotiate by Chester Karrass.
- Bargaining for Advantage: Negotiation Strategies for Reasonable People by G. Richard Shell.

5 - Job Offer Checklist

1. Position
   a. title
   b. location of job
   c. reporting structure
   d. start date

2. Cash Compensation
   a. base salary
      i. amount
      ii. when paid
   b. bonuses
      i. amount
      ii. when paid
      iii. based on what criteria

3. Equity Compensation (may reference additional documents)
   a. form of equity (stock, options, RSUs, etc.)
   b. when awarded
   c. one-time vs. annual grants
   d. vesting schedule
   e. strike price or valuation

4. Benefits (may reference additional documents)
   a. medical, dental insurance
   b. vacation, sick, holiday, paid leave
   c. life insurance, long-term disability
   d. 401K
   e. other

5. Termination
   a. definitions of "with cause" and "without cause"
   b. terms of termination
   c. separation benefits
   d. severance payments

6. Change of Control Provisions (for private companies)
    a. definition of change of control
    b. double trigger provisions (change of control and loss of job)
    c. single trigger provisions (change of control only, no loss of job)

7. Proprietary Information
    a. confidentiality
    b. non-disclosure agreements (NDAs)
    c. invention assignment
    d. non-compete
    e. non-solicitation

8. Dispute Resolution
    a. how, when, where

9. Terms of Acceptance
    a. by when
    b. contingencies (subject to background checks, reference checks, etc.)

6 - Exercise

What would you do in the following situations?

1) You just received an offer for a job you're really excited about, but the offer appears to be below market, and it's less than you've been making over the past several years.

2) You just received an offer for a job you're moderately excited about, and the offer seems way above market, and it's 40% more than you've been making over the past several years.

3) You've been interviewing with Company A for the past few weeks, and you're moving towards an offer, probably within the next week. You're interested in the opportunity, but it's not ideal. You just got a call from a Hiring Manager from Company B whom you met with a few weeks ago. An opportunity has just opened up at Company B, and based on what you know, it sounds much more exciting than the opportunity at Company A.

Notes

Made in the USA
Lexington, KY
26 May 2017